QUEST FOR QUALITY

Improving Basic Skills Instruction in the 1980s

Edited by

Forrest W. Parkay
Sharon O'Bryan
Michael Hennessy
Southwest Texas State University

UNIVERSITY
PRESS OF
AMERICA

LANHAM • NEW YORK • LONDON

CONTENTS

iv

FOREWORD

The papers in this volume are the proceedings of the National Leadership Conference on Basic Skills held January 7-8, 1982, at Southwest Texas State University, San Marcos, Texas. This invitational conference, sponsored by the University's Center for the Study of Basic Skills, provided a forum for national leaders to identify and to discuss promising practices, problems, and solutions in basic skills instruction.

The book is intended for the large number of people who are either interested or actively engaged in improving basic skills instruction: practitioners in elementary, middle, and secondary schools and colleges; basic skills policy makers; university-based researchers and teacher educators; and school administrators. The volume attempts to bring together and to solidify our fundamental knowledge about basic skills instruction as we move into the 1980s.

In spite of dwindling federal support for improving basic skills instruction in our nation's schools, it is clear that much work remains to be done to increase student achievement. The following papers, we feel, provide the strategies for accomplishing this work.

In Part I, Thomas Good details the progress that has been made in classroom research during the past decade and discusses three characteristics of effective teaching: teacher expectations, active teaching, and classroom management. In Part II, Stephen Judy reviews several points of agreement and disagreement in writing research and practice and then makes four recommendations for changes in writing instruction. Beverley Bimes then concludes this section with a teacher's view of improving writing instruction. The improvement of mathematics instruction in the 1980s is discussed in Part III by Shirley Frye and Ross Taylor, both of whom outline a specific agenda for action. In Part IV, Lloyd Kline offers three principles accepted by most reading educators and then posits three statements of need which ought to guide reading instructors. Next, David Pearson recommends that teachers change their questioning strategies and instruction in vocabulary and comprehension skills and that they become more active in modeling and providing feedback to learners. Finally, Rosalinda Barrera explores the complexities of teaching reading to language minority students. In Part V, Barbara Lieb-Brilhart discusses the evolution of oral communication as a basic skill and makes five recommendations for improving oral communication research and instruction. Kenneth Brown then reviews several approaches to instruction in and assessment of oral communication skills. In Part VI, Shirley Jackson and Raymon Bynum outline the roles that the federal and state governments will assume in the basic skills movement in the 1980s. William Bechtol concludes this section by discussing the important contributions that higher education can make to the basic skills effort. In Part VII, Carol Daniels asserts that teachers can influence publishers to produce educational materials that reflect the conference's recommendations in basic skills instruction. In addition, she outlines the criteria for teachers to use in selecting materials. Finally, Forrest Parkay and Sharon O'Bryan comment in their epilogue on the need to keep alive the quest to improve the quality of schooling in the 1980s.

We feel that the following papers represent a significant contribution to our understanding of how to improve basic skills instruction. Furthermore, we hope that these papers will keep alive a serious and sustained dialogue on how to improve the educational lives of all our nation's students.

Southwest Texas State University
San Marcos, Texas
June 1982

Forrest W. Parkay
Sharon O'Bryan
Michael Hennessy

ACKNOWLEDGMENTS

Many people were instrumental in making possible the National Leadership Conference on Basic Skills. The entire staff of the Center for the Study of Basic Skills, under the leadership of co-directors William Bechtol, Robert Northcutt, and Martha Brunson, worked energetically and creatively to put on a successful conference. Essential encouragement, advice, and support were willingly provided by staff members of the U.S. Department of Education and the Texas Education Agency.

Sharon O'Bryan, conference coordinator, was instrumental in organizing and bringing together her colleagues at the University and a national planning committee which consisted of Carl Candoli, Emmet Crawley, Gene Hall, Lloyd Kline, Barbara Lieb-Brilhart, Barbara Little, Leroy Psencik, Charles Suhor, and Ross Taylor. Additional valuable assistance was provided by SWT's Forrest Parkay who organized the small group conference sessions, Lowell Bynum who provided numerous valuable suggestions during the planning phase, and Robert Northcutt, Stinson Worley, Richard Cheatham, and Martha Brunson who chaired general sessions.

Small group discussion sessions were ably facilitated by Betty Moore, Michael Vivion, Michael Hennessy, Mary Olson, John Edgell, and Nancy Grayson. The foregoing group leaders were also assisted by the following who served as group recorders: Robert Northcutt, Marcia Guddemi, Beverly Hardcastle, Marguerite Gillis, and Clifford Ronan.

Because of the participatory approach used in developing the conference's recommendations for basic skills instruction in the 1980s, literally scores of conference participants made contributions which have been included in this volume. Unfortunately, space does not permit the acknowledgment of each of these persons by name. In addition, the resultant quality of the conference was enhanced by the many professional educational organizations which provided the Center staff with the names of key educators to invite.

The papers delivered by conference speakers and the recommendations made in the small group sessions were capably summarized by Forrest Parkay, Nancy Grayson, Robert Northcutt, Stinson Worley, and Sharon O'Bryan.

The success of any national conference is enhanced by administrative backing. In the case of the National Leadership Conference on Basic Skills, essential support was given by Southwest Texas State University President Robert Hardesty and former Vice President for Academic Affairs, Richard Miller. Susan Wittig, Dean of Graduate Studies and Research, and James Garland, Dean of the School of Education, also provided valuable leadership and support.

Special thanks is given to Oscar Dorsey, Dean of Public Service and Adult Continuing Education. He and his staff, especially Betty Fairly, aided tremendously in arranging the details of the conference. In addition, Theodore Keck, Chairman of the Department of Health and Physical Education, willingly provided assistance for this project.

The conference sponsors are also indebted to Mrs. George Bush, wife of Vice President George Bush, who, although unable to attend, gave her wholehearted support to the effort.

The perseverance and competence of Maurine Adamek, secretary for the Center for the Study of Basic Skills, were invaluable throughout all phases of the conference and in the completion of this project. In addition, Department of Education secretaries Paola Kirchoff and Mary Hernandez willingly provided additional help when needed.

Finally, acknowledgment is made to those in the Departments of Education, English, Mathematics, and Speech Communication and Theatre Arts who commented in helpful ways on various parts of this volume.

FOCUS FOR BASIC SKILLS INSTRUCTION IN THE 1980s

Forrest W. Parkay & Sharon O'Bryan
Southwest Texas State University

America's school system is currently striving to meet the complex needs of a society undergoing extensive social and economic change. This system, in an attempt to be responsive to all its constituencies, is overwhelmed with young people from divergent backgrounds.

In recent years the press, educators, students, parents, and employers have complained about the level of literacy within this mix of young people. Pressure to increase achievement in the basic skills (defined in a 1978 U.S. Senate Committee Report as reading, mathematics, and oral and written communication) resulted in a back-to-basics movement that received much attention in the media. Initial support for this movement came from federal monies, though today we are witnessing extensive cutbacks in federal support of basic skills improvement programs.

As we move into the 1980s, then, several questions must be addressed: Where are we, and where are we going with basic skills programs? What are effective programs and practices in basic skills? Finally, what will happen to the strides made in basic skills programs as federal funding dwindles—can we maintain, even extend, our successes?

To answer these questions, educators and basic skills policy makers from nineteen states, the District of Columbia, and three countries convened at Southwest Texas State University on January 7-8, 1982, for the National Leadership Conference on Basic Skills. A Conference Declaration for Basic Skills Instruction in the 1980s, compiled from key points made by the twelve main speakers and the reactions of participants in small group discussions, was developed.

Five recommendations from this declaration stand out as essential to any effort to improve instruction:

- Time must be scheduled for reading, mathematics, and oral and written communication.
- Teachers must expand and develop their teaching skills.
- Relationships among all the basic skills should be explored and taught across the curriculum.
- Research-proven effective practices should be implemented locally even though federal support is diminishing.
- Educators must remember that no simple solutions exist for complex educational problems.

The following conference declaration, presented here in its entirety, offers a sufficiently clear focus for improving instruction in the 1980s. We hope that educators around the country will find this document a useful, pointed synthesis of current, first-rate research and practice in teacher effectiveness, staff development, reading, mathematics, and oral and written communication. The declaration represents, too, a compelling statement that *today* we possess adequate knowledge to begin to improve significantly the educational lives of our nation's students.

CONFERENCE DECLARATION FOR BASIC SKILLS
INSTRUCTION IN THE 1980s

Research-Based Findings on Teacher Effectiveness

- **Effective Teachers Do Have a Measurable, Important Influence on Student Learning.**
Recent research based on classroom observation illustrates convincingly that teachers do have a measurable, important influence on student learning. Researchers, however, need to spend more time working in classrooms in order to formulate more realistic and accurate conceptions of the teacher's role and to determine *how* effective teachers differ from ineffective teachers. Researchers must also work at the local school level to help teachers implement research findings.

- **Teacher Expectations Significantly Influence Student Learning.**
Effective teachers view teaching as a complex job that, despite its difficulties, can be done effectively. They also communicate to their students appropriate expectations—neither too high nor too low.

- **Skills Maintenance Programs Enhance Student Learning.**
Achievement can be improved when previously learned skills are systematically reviewed on a regular basis. A five- to fifteen-minute review every day or every other day is most effective. It is easier to stop students from forgetting than to let them forget and then teach them again. Skills maintenance is an excellent transition activity after recess or lunch or at the beginning of a period. Moreover, a skills maintenance program can be implemented with relatively little inservice training.

- **Active Teaching Results in Increased Student Achievement.**
Teachers who are more active in presenting information, paying attention to the meaning and conceptual development of content, looking for signs of student comprehension and/or confusion, and providing successful practice opportunities appear to have more student achievement gains than do teachers who are less active and rely more upon seatwork and other classroom activities.

- **Classroom Management Affects Student Achievement.**
Classroom management (including the effective use of time, proactive planning, and responding to students' behavior) strongly influences student achievement. There is, however, no list of simple rules that guarantees successful management—effective management varies with the age of students, instructional goals, etc. Still, the concepts and research findings in this area are numerous and useful and should be communicated in teacher education and inservice programs.

- **No Simple Solutions Exist for Complex Educational Problems.**
Educational problems are profoundly complex and, as such, are beyond the simple solutions often proposed. Research has provided some important concepts for analyzing and designing instruction, but these findings cannot be applied to educational settings without first considering the context within which the individual teacher works.

Staff Development

- **Administrators Must Encourage Teachers To Improve Skills Through Inservice and Membership in Professional Organizations.**
Effective teachers must be flexible enough to recognize changes in education and in the world at large. They must look at new learning theories, teaching methods, and student populations and be willing to adapt their teaching to these. Administrators should, therefore, develop and support leadership among teachers and encourage all teachers to participate in professional organizations.

- **Teachers Must Commit Themselves to Continuous Professional Growth.**
Teachers must be encouraged to improve their decision-making skills as they search for their own most effective methods for teaching basic skills. Through increased monitoring and examination of their teaching behaviors, teachers can better understand classroom dynamics and learn when and how to apply research findings.

Oral Communication

- **Explore the Relationship Between Oral and Written Communication Skills.**
Similarities and differences between oral and written communication should be identified and made apparent to teachers and students. The historical canons of invention and arrangement should be common to both oral and written basic skills.

- **Emphasize Oral Communication Instruction.**
Adequate time must be allowed for oral communication in the following six areas: verbal skills, nonverbal skills, interaction skills, critical/evaluative skills, message strategy skills, and functional/situational skills. Curriculum goals must be as clear for oral communication as they are for other subject areas—no longer should oral communication merely provide supportive activities for other language arts.

- **Develop Interactive Methods of Assessment and Performance Measures Which Are Valid, Reliable, and Feasible.**
Federal, state, and local education agencies should develop new methods of assessment that are valid, reliable, and feasible. In addition, these agencies should conduct studies to allay or verify fears that oral communication assessment is too time consuming and costly. The results of the new assessment efforts should be disseminated widely throughout basic skills programs in order to promote alternative means of assessment and to help others avoid duplicating work already done.

- **Develop a National Oral Communication Project Patterned After the National Writing Project.**
Because the National Writing Project has earned acclaim from both educators and the general public, a similar project for oral communication could produce equally valuable results.

Reading

- **Reading Skills Should Be Taught In Context—Not Isolation.**
Students cannot be taught to read outside the context of their expectations, cares, doubts, questions, loves, or hates. Furthermore, teachers should not use the results of one small research study without considering the larger context—the mystery and awe through which any of us at random learns to read.

- **Reading Instruction Should Be Explicitly Structured and Organized.**
  While no specific system of reading instruction works with all students, just about any system works with most if it is structured and organized. Reading teachers need to bring a greater sense of order to their classrooms by knowing exactly what they are trying to do, by letting students in on that knowledge, and by expecting appropriate behavior of them.

- **Questions Asked of Readers Should Be Changed To Promote Better Understanding.**
  Research suggests that it matters a great deal what kinds of questions teachers and teachers' manuals use to determine students' story comprehension. Questions that ask students to predict, to relate the text to prior knowledge, and to evaluate predicted outcomes are superior to more literal and factual questions.

- **Vocabulary Instruction Should Be Changed To Relate More To Students' Present Knowledge and Experience.**
  Instruction that emphasizes where a word fits in a student's present vocabulary is better than methods that emphasize word recognition vocabulary and verbatim definitions. A reader's knowledge of a topic and of the key vocabulary included in a text is a better predictor of comprehension of that text than is any measure of reading ability or achievement.

- **Reading Teachers Should Give Frequent, Direct, and Explicit Instruction for Comprehension Skills.**
  Research suggests that comprehension (though a complex interactive process between the reader and the text) can be taught. Current approaches to comprehension that stress only practice omit a critical element—the teacher acting as a model, demonstrating how to solve problems and showing what clues to look for in the text in order to find solutions. Comprehension activities, then, should include teacher modeling, guided practice, and regular corrective responses from the teacher.

Writing

- **Writing Programs Must Be Based on Frequent, Authentic Writing Experience.**
  Writing is a learn-by-doing skill, and therefore frequent writing practice is necessary for both basic and advanced students. The question for the 1980s is not whether Johnny and Jane have mastered mandated objectives or hierarchical patterns of discrete language skills, but how often they write, to whom, for what purposes, and under what kind of professional guidance.

- **Writing Must Be Part of All Classes, Not Just English/Language Arts.**
  Writing-across-the-curriculum must be developed and implemented by English teachers so that students will write in all classes. Research in the language learning process shows that composition is not merely the putting down of ideas preformed in the writer's head; the writing process is inextricably bound to discovery, to gaining knowledge—knowledge of the world and of the self. Writing is both a liberal art and a skill; as such, it is absolutely essential for learning in all disciplines. Therefore, the teaching of writing cannot and should not be exclusively the domain of English teachers.

4

- **All English Teachers and Content Area Teachers Must Expand and Develop Their Writing Skills.**
  The success of the National Writing Project shows that the way to improve writing instruction in the schools is to help teachers educate themselves about current methodology, not to threaten them with standardized tests. Inservice is expensive, of course, but it can be effective. If the money now used for testing programs were redirected toward well-conceived inservice, there would be enough money to reeducate all willing teachers, with some left over for modest, well-conceived testing programs.

- **Composition Teachers Must Be Given More Satisfactory Teaching Conditions, Including Manageable Class Sizes and Loads.**
  For over two decades the National Council of Teachers of English has advocated class loads for secondary English teachers not to exceed one hundred students and four classes. But during those decades we have seen class sizes and loads in most states increase, not decrease. Even drawing on contemporary peer-editing techniques, no teacher can teach writing effectively to massive numbers of students. If schools are serious about improving writing instruction, they must pay attention to manageable class sizes and loads.

Mathematics

- **Identify Mathematics as an Essential Basic Skill.**
  Each school district should have a written policy that identifies mathematics as an essential basic skill. This policy should identify various mathematical skills, not just computation, as basic and should support a strong mathematical program. The program should be supported through adequate resources and should actively involve administrators, teachers, students, parents, and the community.

- **Emphasize and Identify Basic Skills Areas in Mathematics.**
  Each basic skills program should include at least the ten areas identified in the National Council of Supervisors of Mathematics' Position Paper on Basic Mathematical Skills: problem solving; applying mathematics to everyday situations; alertness to reasonableness of results; estimation and approximation; appropriate computation skills; geometry; measurement; tables, charts, and graphs; using mathematics to predict; and computer literacy. The National Council of Teachers of Mathematics' *Agenda for Action: Recommendation for School Mathematics for the 1980s* supports such a position and places special emphasis on problem solving.

- **Emphasize Mathematics Skills for Career Alternatives.**
  The National Council of Teachers of Mathematics recommends at least three years of mathematics for grades 9 through 12 in order to give students a wide choice of career alternatives. The Council also encourages mathematics instruction during the senior year to maintain continuity of learning and development of potential. The diverse needs of the school population in the face of new and developing fields require a lifelong learning of skills.

- **Incorporate Available Technology into the Mathematics Program.**
  Mathematics programs should take full advantage of calculators and computers at all levels. Used effectively and in a variety of ways, these devices can enhance learning. Students need calculator and computer literacy to function in today's rapidly changing scientific and computer oriented society.

PART I:
TEACHER EFFECTIVENESS

RESEARCH ON TEACHING:
SOME IMPORTANT AREAS OF PROGRESS

Thomas L. Good
University of Missouri

Introduction

This paper will describe the progress that has been made in classroom research in the past decade, particularly in the area of basic skills instruction. We know considerably more about classroom teaching than we did a decade ago. In 1970 the accumulated knowledge about the effects of classroom processes on student achievement was weak and contradictory. Although we still have much to learn, the literature on basic skills instruction in reading and mathematics in elementary schools has moved from a state of confusion to a point where experimental studies can be designed upon a data base. Later, I will return to a discussion of what we have learned from recent research; however, it is important first to examine historical factors.

School Critics: Simple Solutions

In the late 1960s it was popular to criticize teachers and schooling. Indeed, following the publication of the Coleman et al. findings (1966) and the initial disappointing results of Head Start research, there were increasing doubts about whether teachers affected students' learning, and financial support for education decreased. Unfortunately, the charge that teaching made little difference in students' learning was not based upon classroom observation. Despite the willingness of critics to design new programs for solving the "problems" that confronted American education in the late 1960s, there was little information for describing what took place in classrooms (Schwab, 1968).

In a comprehensive review of the major individualization techniques used in reading instruction during the 1900s, Artley noted that despite the many desirable features of each *new* approach, the effectiveness of any single approach for teaching reading is seriously limited. Artley argues that any program helps the reading problems of *some* students but creates (or at least fails to respond to) difficulties for other students.

I believe that in the past, educators have moved (often with the best of intentions) from fad to fad because the field did not possess sufficient observational data to indicate how complex teaching is or to illustrate the various tradeoffs that occur in any teaching situation. I agree with Artley that innovations proposed in education (the activity movement, individualization and openness, back to basics) tend to be so sweeping that they substitute one set of problems for another.

Benefits of Educational Research

In the 1970s much observational research was collected in classrooms. These data have illustrated that general, universal theories of teaching may be unobtainable because the characteristics of good teaching vary as the context (e.g., age, ability of students) of teaching and the educational goals change (Brophy and Evertson, 1976). In part, observational research in classrooms increased because researchers were becoming more dissatisfied with theory developed only in laboratory settings. Furthermore, some investigators were presenting data which indicated that classrooms were much more complex and learning much more problematic than previously believed (e.g., Jackson, 1968; Smith & Geoffrey, 1968).

Although it is impossible to review specific methodological advances here (see Brophy, 1979 for a good review), it is important to emphasize that advances in the understanding of classrooms in the 1970s occurred not only because of *more* observation but also because of better quantitative and qualitative observational procedures and more adequately selected samples. Although there are many reasons why observational procedures were improved in the 1970s, gains were achieved largely because of the willingness of the National Institute of Education to encourage sophisticated research in ongoing classrooms and because scholars were beginning to provide conceptual direction to the field (e.g., Rosenshine & Furst, 1971; Dunkin & Boddle, 1974).

New Information About Classrooms

Classroom observation has revealed much information about classroom phenomena that was not widely known a decade ago. Past critics of education often described classrooms as though there was no meaningful variation in teacher behavior or in school practices (to describe one school was to describe them all). Depending upon the critic, all schools were "too controlled" or "too haphazard." However, data collected in the past ten years illustrate that some classrooms are "under managed" and others "over managed" (e.g., Leinhardt et al., 1979). Some teachers treat high and low achievers differently (Brophy & Good, 1979), but in other classrooms students believed by teachers to be less capable than other students receive equitable or even more favorable treatment than students believed to be more capable (Brophy & Good, 1974; Good et al., 1980).

Despite the fact that school critics explicitly suggest (or implicitly imply—when only one solution is offered) that teachers (and schools) behave in similar ways, there is now compelling evidence at the elementary school level to illustrate that this is not the case. Formal studies of classrooms (e.g., Bossert, 1979) illustrate that classrooms often appear similar but place different task demands upon students, and that other classrooms which appear dissimilar actually place similar learning demands upon students. In other words, elementary school teachers structure and organize learning tasks in different ways.

Other research also indicates that teachers behave in different ways. In addition to the fact that teachers vary in how they *interact* with students (e.g., who vary in sex, ability, and ethnicity), teachers have also been found to vary widely in how they use *praise* (Brophy, 1981: Some teachers use praise contingently; others noncontingently) and in how they use *time* (e.g., Roseshine, 1980: Some teachers may spend twice as much time on a subject as another teacher in the same grade at the same school). Furthermore, teachers also vary in how they *use* time in a particular subject area. For example, Good and Grouws (1977) found that teachers differ widely in how much time they spend discussing the meaning of the mathematics lesson and in the time they allow students to do independent seatwork.

From this naturalistic study of mathematics classes in elementary schools, Doug Grouws and I concluded that in many classrooms (but not all) there is too little active teaching focused upon the *meaning* of the lesson and too much attention to drill. Other investigators have reached similar conclusions (too little attention in many classrooms to comprehension and meaning) in the area of reading (e.g., Durkin, 1978-79; Leinhardt, et al., 1981).

These are only a *few* of the ways in which observational research in the 1970s indicates that teachers vary in behavior and organization. Such findings suggest that "single answers" are difficult to justify because instructional "problems" vary widely from classroom to classroom.

Teachers Make A Difference

In addition to the fact that teachers vary in their behavior, there is increasing evidence that some types of variation are related to different levels of *mean* classroom achievement. Recent observational research provides solid evidence that teachers teaching similar pupils under similar circumstances often behave in different ways and that these differences in teacher behavior can be associated with differential learning gains. Furthermore, research has demonstrated that teachers can be trained to improve mean student achievement in elementary school and junior high *mathematics* (Good & Grouws, 1981) and *reading* (Anderson, Evertson & Brophy, 1979; Stallings, 1979, 1980).

Such findings are important and useful to teachers; however, some students have benefited more from certain instructional techniques which experimental (trained) teachers used than other types of students. In addition, the type of school organization and type of teacher also appear to mediate the effects of training. Similar findings are, of course, not uncommon in the change literature (as the work of Gene Hall and his colleagues at the University of Texas has illustrated).

Still, I want to emphasize that in the 1970s research produced evidence that teachers make an important and measurable difference in students' learning, and we have begun to identify some clues about teaching strategies associated with these differences. Also, recent research which has examined school processes (unlike earlier research which focused on non-observational variables—like the number of books in the school library) has provided reasonable *correctional* evidence that some schools have more positive effects on student achievement than other schools (e.g., Rutter et al., 1979).

How Teachers Make A Difference

I do not intend to provide detailed accounts of recent classroom effectiveness studies in this paper. However, I want to discuss three characteristics of successful teaching: positive teacher expectations, active teaching, and effective classroom management (when successful teaching is equated with students' achievement on stardardized tests).

Teacher Expectations

Brophy and Good (1974) have shown that teachers vary widely in the extent to which they behave differentially toward students they believe to be high and low achievers. However, differential treatment of students cannot necessarily be equated with poor teaching. Teachers can expect *too much* or *too little* in their instructional interactions with students (Good & Brophy, 1978), and there are times when teachers probably need to treat students differently if they are to stimulate optimal learning (Bank, Biddle & Good, 1980).

Still, it is important to note several replicated findings of ways in which some teachers behave in a potentially negative manner toward low achievers. Good and Brophy (1980) report the following behaviors:
1. Seating low students farther from the teacher and/or seating lows in a group;
2. Paying less attention to lows in academic situations;
3. Calling on lows less often to answer classroom questions or to make public demonstrations;
4. Waiting less time for lows to answer questions;
5. Not staying with lows in failure situations (providing clues, asking follow-up questions);

8

6. Criticizing lows more frequently than highs for incorrect public responses;
7. Praising lows less frequently than highs after successful public responses;
8. Praising lows more frequently than highs for marginal or inadequate public responses;
9. Providing low-achieving students with less accurate and less detailed feedback than highs;
10. Failing to provide lows with feedback about their responses more frequently than highs;
11. Demanding less work and effort from lows than from highs;
12. Interrupting the performance of low achievers more frequently than that of high achievers.

The list of teaching behaviors presented above can only guide teachers' and supervisors' efforts as they analyze classrooms. However, if many of these behaviors are present in a classroom, student opportunity to learn and motivation for learning would probably be reduced, especially if low students are presented with *less content* and *less opportunity* to learn.

In *correlational* interview work with teachers (who varied notably in their ability to obtain student achievement), Evertson and Brophy found that teachers who were obtaining achievement gains from students believed that they could teach and viewed the task of teaching as a complex but "doable" job. In contrast, teachers who obtained lower levels of student achievement were more ambivalent about whether they could teach certain students. It may be that appropriate expectations play an important mediation role in helping teachers to develop active communication skills.

Teachers who hold appropriate expectations seem to be willing to continue to work with students who have initial learning difficulties. They appear to expect that students can learn and that their job as a teacher is to find a way to promote such learning. This appropriate expectations variable is similar to some of the process measures that Rutter et al. (1979) found to differentiate more and less effective schools (e.g., an emphasis on school learning; high teacher expectations that students will learn).

Although the antecedent factors that precede the development of appropriate teacher expectations are unclear, there is abundant correlational evidence to associate consistently appropriate teacher expectations for student learning and actual student achievement.

I (Good, 1981b) have also argued that within a school year low achievers may be asked to adjust to more varied teacher behavior than high-achieving students. Many low achievers have different teachers in addition to their regular classroom teacher, such as remedial math, reading, or speech teachers. Although there are no detailed reports on how remedial teachers differ in their instructional behavior from regular classroom teachers (if indeed they do), multiple teachers increase the chances for students to encounter different expectations and varied instructional behaviors. Others too have commented upon this problem. For example, a recent report by the Rand Corporation (reported in *Education Week*, December 21, 1981) notes that in some schools students are exposed to different and conflicting curricula in regular and special classrooms. Ironically, it seems that schooling practices may require students who have the least adaptive capacity to make the greatest adjustment as they move from class to class.

Unfortunately, there is little research evidence directly examining the teacher behavior that students receive as they move from one grade to the next, and/or the consistency between the behavior of regular classroom teachers and remedial teachers. However, indirect evidence suggests that great discontinuities in behavioral

9

performance expectations exist for some students as they move from classroom to classroom or from school to school. These differences in role expectations may make it difficult for students to understand what is expected of them and, indeed, may lead to student uncertainty about the value of a particular subject matter, because teachers have different beliefs about how the subject should be taught.

Implications, Suggestions

Observational data have suggested the "problem" varies from classroom to classroom. Some teachers assign lows material that is too difficult but other teachers assign content that is too easy (this appears to be the more common problem). Considering this *variability*, rules like "increase the number of times lows are called on and the frequency of their praise will do more harm than good (i.e., some teachers are already utilizing these techniques appropriately and for them this advice would have dysfunctional effects).

The variables that affect teaching and learning are numerous, complex, and interrelated. *Knowledge* related to teacher expectation effects is therefore best imparted to teachers along with *judgmental* and *decision-making* skills about its appropriate use rather than presenting teachers with a list of behaviors they need to perform. An important policy step would be the transformation of existing knowledge about teacher and student expectation effects into an organized curriculum (readings, videotapes) that causes increased teacher awareness of issues involved in forming and communicating low expectations. This curriculum would also enable teachers to develop skills for applying such knowledge in various contexts and problem situations. Fortunately, some work that may encourage teachers to develop and to use decision-making skills generally (Amerel, 1981) and specifically in the area of teacher expectations (Good & Brophy, 1978) has been completed.

In inservice settings, the chance to observe more frequently in other classrooms can provide teachers with an excellent means for understanding that low achievers can learn and can help teachers to identify numerous strategies for interacting with all students, but especially with low achievers (Good, in press). When teachers see low-achieving students respond in ways which they did not feel were possible, they are likely to reevaluate their expectations and behavior toward low achievers.

As I have argued elsewhere (Good, in progress), if inservice work in this area is to be successful, efforts need to be made to improve principals' observational skills as well as their abilities for establishing *staff development* activities for instructional development (not evaluation). Unfortunately, despite the commonly asserted belief that one of a principal's main duties is to provide instructional leadership, many principals and some curriculum supervisors do not have the skills necessary for this task. Most principals take only limited course work in curriculum and instruction and have little expertise or appreciation for helping teachers to become more skillful in controlling their expectations about students or subject matter. More course work in these areas for administrators would seem essential if the advantages of classroom observation are to be realized.

Teacher Education

Information about ways in which some teachers differ in their behavior toward high- and low-achieving students should be included in all teacher education programs. I do not know to what extent this information is presently contained in such curricula. However, informal contact with teachers suggests that many teachers do not know how to monitor and/or analyze their interactions with different types of students. In short, they do not have a *model* for considering or explaining how and why low expectations might be communicated in the classroom.

Available evidence indirectly indicates that lows receive more varied classroom teaching behaviors than highs. It seems plausible that part of this variation is due to the lack of teacher agreement about how to respond to student failure. Teacher education programs could play a valuable role by helping prospective teachers to understand that a degree of failure will be present in any teaching situation (learning occurs in stages and re-teaching is often necessary). Programs should develop teachers' skills so that they can interpret student failure as a challenge, and should provide teachers with better conceptualized strategies for responding to student failure.

Teacher education programs need to create role definitions which specify that the teacher is there primarily to teach actively, and that failure calls for reteaching rather than rationalization. Methods classes should stress *diagnosis* and remediation following failure. Teacher education programs need more emphasis upon adapting instruction after initial teaching. Too much of the information in these programs implies that learning is non-problematic if certain methods are faithfully applied. Inappropriate expectations may exist for some teachers because teacher education programs in the 1960s and 1970s emphasized that if one plans well (the behavioral objective movement), success follows.

Instruction that encourages prospective teachers to think about the need to coordinate their beliefs and behaviors (e.g., reactions to failure, criteria for evaluating student work) with the beliefs and practices of other teachers in the same school is also needed. Variation among teachers in beliefs and behavior may often have desirable effects on some students, especially when teachers *explain* the reasons for change (. . . . last year different criteria were used for grading your composition papers; this year emphasis is placed upon X because . . . .). However, unexplained discrepancies that exist between classrooms could negatively affect some students' motivation and understanding (especially low achievers).

As argued elsewhere (Good, in progress), the literature on teacher effectiveness was so dismal in the late 1960s, many training programs may have inadvertently reduced teacher motivation by stressing the difficulties associated with teaching. Teaching is a very tough, demanding, but doable job (Good & Brophy, 1978, 1980). Unrealistically high or low expectations about teaching and, in particular, teachers' ability to influence low achievers, may have subtle negative effects upon teachers' subsequent classroom behavior.

At present virtually no information exists about the expectations of beginning teachers. Experimental research on this issue is needed. I emphasize that most research on teacher expectations has involved a correlational examination of the relationship between teachers' beliefs about students, their verbal behavior toward students perceived to be high and low achievers, and student achievement. More comprehensive assessments are needed of non-verbal behaviors through which teachers may communicate inappropriate expectations to students (e.g., comments written on students' papers).

Active Teaching

Research on teacher effectiveness has not yielded specific guidelines about *how* to teach, but it has provided clear evidence that teachers can and do make a difference. As reflected in many recent articles, the current Zeitgeist appears to be a call for increasing the *quantity* of teaching (more time for basic skills instruction, more "time on task"). However, the most evident message that recent research presents to me is that the *quality* of teaching needs attention. Our initial naturalistic study of more and less effective teachers indicated that effective teachers were

11

distinguished by *how* they taught mathematics and not by the amount of time they spent on mathematics. Teachers who obtained higher gains made better use of time and obtained more student involvement, but they also maintained a good balance between theory and practice (conceptualization, application, and drill).

I believe the most important implication which teacher effectiveness research has for teacher education is that teachers need to be active in their teaching. Teachers who are more active in presenting information, pay attention to the meaning and conceptual development of content, look for signs of student comprehension and/or confusion, and provide successful practice opportunities appear to have more achievement gains than do teachers who are less active and who rely more upon seatwork and other classroom activities. Most teacher effectiveness research has been conducted in elementary classrooms; however, in secondary mathematics there are reasonably consistent data as well (e.g., Evertson, Anderson, Anderson, & Brophy, 1980; Weber, 1978).

I prefer the concept of active teaching rather than the term "direct instruction" (which has been used to describe the pattern of behavior of teachers who obtain higher-than-expected achievement from students) because it represents a broader concept of teaching than does the existing research base. In active teaching, the initial style can be inductive or deductive, and student learning can be self-initiated or teacher-initiated (especially if thorough critique and synthesis activities follow student learning attempts). Active teaching also connotes a broader philosophical base (active teaching can occur in classrooms using a variety of classroom organizational structures), and should become somewhat less direct as students become more mature and instructional goals become concerned with affective and process outcomes (Good, 1979). Also, active teaching techniques can be applied in both teacher-led instruction as well as in student team learning/instruction (e.g., Peterson, Janicki, & Swing, 1980; Slavin, 1981; Webb, 1977).

Active teaching provides an important instructional construct for characterizing the teaching role. With the apparent growing pressure for teachers to function as classroom managers rather than as instructors, more emphasis should be placed in teacher education programs upon helping teachers to understand active teaching. As I have emphasized elsewhere (Good, in progress), and in the section of this paper on teacher expectation implications, the dissemination of this knowledge should be in a *decision-making* context that helps teachers to adapt the concept to particular types of content and students. The development of videotapes that illustrate the concept of active teaching in real classrooms would be particularly important. Clearly, the effects of such simulation activities upon teachers' judicious use of the concept in real classrooms should be assessed. Unfortunately, there are very few studies on how research findings and concepts can be taught in a decision-making format. Such research is badly needed.

Classroom Management

Classroom management (including time utilization, proactive planning, and responding to students' behavior) was an active and productive research area in the 1970s. I give less attention to this topic because of space limitations placed upon the paper and because relevant concepts and findings are readily available elsewhere (e.g., Good & Brophy, 1978).

In the 1960s classroom management was often defined as classroom discipline and considerable emphasis was placed upon what to do *after* students misbehaved. Research initiated by Kounin (1970) and validated and expanded by a number of researchers in the past few years has strongly illustrated that good classroom managers are not sharply differentiated in terms of how they react to student misbehavior. Rather, good classroom managers utilize techniques which *prevent* misbehavior by eliciting student cooperation in general and involvement in assigned work specifically. Much is now known about these general managerial principles and about proactive teaching behavior. Kounin's concepts (e.g., "withitness") are conceptually helpful.

As I have noted in previous studies (Good, 1979; 1981a), teachers' managerial abilities have been found to relate positively to student achievement in *every* process-product study conducted to date. Many classroom management principles *appear* to be applicable to a variety of teaching situations (for details, see Good & Brophy, 1980). It seems that teacher managerial skills are necessary if reasonable pupil achievement is to occur, and these concepts and principles should be included in preservice teacher training programs.

There are many other sources that emphasize classroom management principles and/or present Kounin's concepts. For example, one entire yearbook of the National Society for the Study of Education (Duke, 1979) is devoted to classroom management. Another good source is *Looking in Classrooms* (Good & Brophy, 1978). This text emphasizes Kounin's distinction between reactive and proactive classroom management and there is considerable discussion of how teachers can prevent problems.

Another source of information on translating classroom management research into classroom practice is the research program on classroom management (COET) at the University of Texas Research and Development Center for Teacher Education. This program was conceptualized and coordinated for several years by Carolyn Evertson and is now headed by Edmund Emmer. The COET program has been active in testing previous concepts related to classroom management (especially those of Kounin) as well as in generating new knowledge. This program has produced convincing evidence that it is possible to describe how more and less able managers differ in their behavior and has illustrated that these managerial strategies can be taught to other teachers.

To reiterate, because of limits on the length of this paper, I could do little more than recognize classroom management as an active and important research area. The interested reader can seek detailed information elsewhere (e.g., Good & Brophy, 1978). However, I want to emphasize that the practical value of classroom management research is at the conceptual and decision-making level. There is no list of simple rules that guarantees successful management if followed (effective management varies with the age of students, instructional goals, etc.). Still, the concepts and research findings in this area are numerous and useful and such knowledge should be communicated in teacher education programs.

Summary and Conclusions

There is now clear evidence that teachers make a measurable and important difference in students' learning (at least in some curriculum areas and for some important educational goals). Research has not yielded guidelines for successful teaching, but it does provide important constructs that teachers can use in studying (and perhaps modifying) their teaching. Research on teacher effectiveness needs to be disseminated in ways which encourage teachers to creatively adapt research findings in their own instructional situations.

I believe that there are now sufficient data to suggest that educators' perceptions of low achievers' learning potential are often too low. Furthermore, there is evidence that lows can and do benefit from active teaching. Teachers can err by having too high expectations and by constructing too demanding assignments; however, in general low achievers are more likely to suffer from too little stimulation and teaching (e.g., too little emphasis upon meaning, unduly repetitious assignments, etc.). Information about the learning potential of students perceived to be low achievers needs to be disseminated to teachers and more active inservice training should concern more adequate ways for teaching low achieving students. Such information needs to be presented in a way that stimulates reflection and analysis, because there are no simple rules that apply in all situations.

One particularly good way to allow teachers and teachers in training to develop more appropriate role expectations is to increase their opportunities for observing other teachers (Good & Brophy, 1978; Good, in press). In terms of expectations for low achievement students, the opportunity to observe and talk with teachers who are successful with low students would be a direct and important way to encourage more active teaching of such students.

Another more general use of classroom observation would be to allow teachers to visit teachers who use teaching styles that differ from their own. Opportunities to observe other teachers would help to break down the physical isolation that is often a part of the teaching profession.

As I have stated elsewhere (Good, in press), another possible gain from classroom observation is coordination of instructional programs within a school. Although there is no reason to expect uniform teaching practices in a school (and many good reasons to accept and to encourage diversity in teaching style), occasionally the discrepancy between how teachers present a subject is so great that it may cause some students great difficulty.

For a variety of reasons, I believe that more opportunity for observing other teachers will help many teachers to think more seriously about their classroom behavior and its effects on students. Obviously, this is an important step if teachers are to creatively adapt research findings and the practices of other teachers to their own teaching situations. For too long, teachers have been encouraged to use "generalized solutions." We now have data which show that classrooms are so complex that recommendations have to be adjusted to particular settings.

Another area that merits much research attention is teacher education. Elsewhere (Good, in progress), I have noted that little is known about the content, beliefs, and skills that teacher education programs communicate to prospective teachers. In particular, there is little information about how teacher education programs help teachers in training to develop skills for interpreting research and for adapting what is known about instruction to the contexts in which they will teach. Are teachers given inconsistent facts and beliefs or are they helped to develop a comprehensive framework for assessing different value perspectives and for developing consistent personal teaching philosophies? It is important to assess how teacher education programs help teachers to define their instructional roles and their relationships to low achieving students. Many teacher education programs could add important content to their curricula in order to improve the observational skills of teachers and their ability to use information gained through observation to adapt instruction as necessary (Amarel, 1981; Good & Brophy, 1978). Recent research evidence has helped to substantiate what classroom teachers have always known, that to do an *effective* job, teachers must possess ability, skills, and work very hard. Considering the demands of teaching, many teacher education programs should require teachers to demonstrate that they can successfully use principles and concepts in actual classroom situations.

Finally, I should emphasize that educators too often overreact to existing problems and such exaggerated responses almost guarantee that new problems will be created. We have developed some important new knowledge about teaching in basic skill subjects; however, such information has to be applied judiciously and in a decision-making format if it is to have a positive impact upon American education.*

*In preparing this paper, the author in a few places has adapted some material from his other recent writings on the topic (Good, in progress; in press; 1981a; and 1981b). The author would also like to acknowledge the general support received from the Center for Research in Social Behavior, University of Missouri-Columbia and Terry Brown, Janice Meiburger and Pat Shanks for typing the manuscript. Furthermore, the helpful editorial suggestions made by Gail Hinkel are acknowledged.

REFERENCES

Amarel, M. *Literacy: The personal dimension*. A paper presented at the annual meeting of the American Educational Research Association, Los Angeles, April 1981.

Anderson, L., Evertson, C., & Brophy, J. An experimental study of effective teaching in first-grade reading groups. *Elementary School Journal*, 1979, *79*(4), 193-223.

Andros, K., & Freeman, D. *The effects of three kinds of feedback on math teaching performance*. A paper presented at the annual meeting of the American Educational Research Association, Los Angeles, April 1981.

Artley, A. Individual differences and reading instruction. *Elementary School Journal*, 1981, *82*, 143-151.

Bank, B., Biddle, B., and Good, T. Sex roles, classroom instruction, and reading achievement. *Journal of Educational Psychology*, 1980, *72*, 119-132.

Bossert, S. Task and social relationships in classrooms: A study of classroom organization and its consequences. American Sociological Association, *Arnold and Caroline Rose Monograph Series*. New York: Cambridge University Press, 1979.

Brophy, J. Teacher behavior and its effects. *Journal of Educational Psychology*, 1979, *71*, 733-750.

Brophy, J. On praising effectively. *Elementary School Journal*, 1981, *81*, 269-278.

Brophy, J., & Evertson, C. *Learning from teaching: A developmental perspective*. Boston: Allyn & Bacon, 1976.

Brophy, J., & Good, T. Teachers' communication of differential expectations for children's classroom performance: Some behavioral data. *Journal of Educational Psychology*, 1970, *61*, 365-374.

Brophy, J., & Good, T. *Teacher-student relationships: Causes and consequences*. New York: Holt, Rinehart and Winston, 1974.

Carew, J., & Lightfoot, S. *Beyond bias*. Cambridge: Harvard University Press, 1979.

Coleman, J., Campbell, E., Hobson, C., McPartland, J., Mood, A., Weinfield, F., & York, R. *Equality of educational opportunity*. Washington, D.C.: Superintendent of Documents, U.S. Government Printing Office, 1966.

Doyle, W. Classroom task and students' abilities. In P. Peterson & H. Walberg (Eds.), *Research on teaching: Concepts, findings, and implications*. Berkeley, Calif.: McCutchan Publishing Corporation, 1979.

Duke, D. (Ed.), *Classroom management. The 78th yearbook of the National Society for the Study of Education* (Part II). Chicago: University of Chicago Press, 1979.

Dunkin, M., & Biddle, B. *The study of teaching*. New York: Holt, Rinehart and Winston, 1974.

Durkin, D. What classroom observations reveal about reading comprehension instruction. *Reading Research Quarterly*, 1978-79, *14*, 481-533.

Ebmeier, H., & Good, T. The effects of instructing teachers about good teaching on the mathematics achievement of fourth graders. *American Educational Research Journal*, 1979, *16*, 1-16.

Ebmeier, H., Good, T., & Grouws, D. *Comparisons of ATI findings across two large-scale experimental studies in elementary education*. A paper presented at the American Educational Research Association Annual Conference, Boston, April 1980.

Evertson, C. Differences in instructional activities in average- and low-achieving junior high English and math classes. *Elementary School Journal*, in press.

Evertson, C., Anderson, C., Anderson, L., & Brophy, J. Relationships between classroom behaviors and student outcomes in junior high mathematics and English classes. *American Educational Research Journal*, 1980, *17*, 43-60.

Gage, N., & Giaconia, R. *The causal connection between teaching practices and student achievement: Recent experiments based on correlational findings* (Tech. Rep.). Stanford, Calif.: Stanford University, Center for Educational Research at Stanford, 1980.

Good, T. *Classroom research*. In progress. (This chapter was prepared at the request of the National Institute of Education). The writing of the chapters in this series is being coordinated by Lee Shulman and Gary Sykes, and it is anticipated that the series will be published in book form in 1982).

Good, T. *Classroom observation: Potential and problems*. In press. (Part of a book on classroom evaluation being compiled and printed at Phi Delta Kappa, Bloomington, Indiana).

Good, T. *Classroom research: What we know and what we need to know*. A paper prepared for the Teacher

Education Program Division (Dr. Gary Griffin, Director) at the Research and Development Center for Teacher Education. Austin, Texas, November 1981a.

Good, T. Teacher effectiveness in the elementary school: What we know about it now. *Journal of Teacher Education*, 1979, *30*, 52-64.

Good, T. A decade of research on teacher expectations. *Journal of Educational Leadership*, 1981b, *38*, 415-423.

Good, T., & Brophy, J. *Looking in classrooms* (2nd ed.). New York: Harper and Row, 1978.

Good, T., & Brophy, J. *Educational psychology: A realistic approach* (2nd ed.). New York: Holt, Rinehart and Winston, 1980.

Good, T., Cooper, H., & Blakey, S. Classroom interaction as a function of teacher expectations, student sex, and time of year. *Journal of Educational Psychology*, 1980, *72*, 378-386.

Good, T., & Grouws, D. *Experimental research in secondary mathematics classrooms: Working with teachers*. Final Report of National Institute of Education Grant NIE-G-79-0103. Columbia, Missouri, May 1981.

Good, T., & Grouws, D. Teaching effects: A process-product study in fourth-grade mathematics classrooms. *Journal of Teacher Education*, 1977, *28*, 49-54.

Good, T., & Grouws, D. The Missouri mathematics effectiveness project: An experimental study in fourth grade classrooms. *Journal of Educational Psychology*, 1979, *71*, 355-362.

Jackson, P. *Life in classrooms*. New York: Holt, Rinehart, and Winston, 1968.

Janicki, C., & Peterson, P. Aptitude-treatment interaction effects of variations in direct instruction. *American Educational Research Journal*, 1981, *18*, 63-82.

Keziah, R. Implementing instructional behaviors that make a difference. *Centroid* (North Carolina Council of Teachers of Mathematics), 1980, *6*, 2-4.

Kounin, J. *Discipline and group management in classrooms*. New York: Holt, Rinehart and Winston, 1970.

Leinhardt, G., Seewald, A., & Engel, M. Learning what's taught: Sex differences in instruction. *Journal of Educational Psychology*, 1979, *71*, 432-439.

Leinhardt, G., Zigmond, N., & Cooley, W. Reading instruction and its effects. *American Educational Research Journal*, 1981, *18*, 343-361.

Peterson, P., Janicki, T., & Swing, S. *Individual characteristics and children's learning in large-group and small-group approaches: Study II* (Tech. Rep. No. 561). Madison, Wis.: University of Wisconsin, Wisconsin Research and Development Center for Individualized Schooling, October 1980.

Rosenshine, B. Content, time, and direction instruction. In P. Peterson & H. Walberg (Eds.), *Research on teaching: Concepts, findings, and implications*. Berkeley, Calif.: McCutchan Publishing Corporation, 1979.

Rosenshine, B. How time is spent in elementary classrooms. In C. Denham & A. Lieberman (Eds.), *Time to learn*. Washington, D.C.: U.S. Department of Education, 1980.

Rosenshine, B., & Furst, N. Research on teacher performance criteria in B. Smith (Ed.), *Research in Teacher Education*. Englewood Cliffs, N.J.: Prentice-Hall, 1971.

Rutter, M., Maughan, B., Mortimore, P., Ouston, J., & Smith, A. *Fifteen thousand hours: Secondary schools and their effects on children*. Cambridge: Harvard University Press, 1979.

Schwab, J. The practical: A language for curriculum. *School Review*, November 1969, 1-23.

Slavin, R. A case study of psychological research affecting classroom practice: Student team learning. *Elementary School Journal*, 1981, *82*, 5-17.

Smith, L., & Geoffrey, W. *The complexities of an urban classroom: An analysis toward a general theory of teaching*. New York: Holt, Rinehart and Winston, 1968.

Stallings, J. Allocated academic learning time revisited, or beyond time on task. *Educational Researcher*, 1980, *9*(11), 11-16.

Stallings, J., Needels, M., & Stayrook, N. *How to change the process of teaching basic reading skills in secondary schools: Phase II and Phase III*, Final Report. Menlo Park, Calif.: SRI International, 1979.

Webb, N. *Learning in individual and small-group settings* (Tech. Rep. No. 7). Stanford, Calif.: Stanford University, School of Education, Aptitude Research Project, 1977.

Weber, E. The effect of learning environment on learner involvement and achievement. *Journal of Teacher Education*, 1978, *29*, 81-85.

PART II: WRITING

RECENT RESEARCH AND NEW DIRECTIONS
IN THE TEACHING OF WRITING

Stephen N. Judy
Michigan State University

Perhaps no area of education has attracted the attention of the media more regularly in the past decade than the teaching of writing. Ever since *Newsweek*, prompted by the announcement of the SAT test score decline, published its "Why Johnny Can't Write" thematic issue in 1975, the local and national press have been filled with stories about the writing deficiencies of Johnny and his sister Jane, characteristically illustrated with samples of student writing that is incoherent and badly spelled, often accompanied by the laments of teachers, parents, and popular media personalities about the "withering away" of the English language at the hands and in the mouths of the current generation of schoolchildren. English/language arts teachers have come in for their share of the blame, and I think it is fair to say that the national impression of English teachers is one of incompetence, of people who have somehow thrown away all standards, who have surrendered to some sort of new wave permissivism, and who, above all, are ignorant of sensible ways to drill writing skills into youngsters.

Predictably, the English teaching profession has responded to the charges and insinuations. Among other things, a number of articulate and well-informed writers have pointed out that a "crisis" in writing is not new and was not discovered by either *Newsweek* or Educational Testing Service.[1] Parents and educators have been concerned about the quality of writing and the quality of writing instruction ever since composition became a part of the school curriculum in the mid-nineteenth century. Nor does the pervasive popular notion of an absolute decay in literacy skills hold up under close examination. Though test scores have declined—often for sociological rather than educational reasons—there is no overwhelming evidence (other than hearsay and media reports) to suggest that Johnny and Jane write any worse than did their parents or their grandparents. Indeed, it may be that the writing skills of the current generation came under close scrutiny because, in contrast to mom's day and grandpa's day, teachers are making a concerted effort to teach literacy to *all* children, not just those select few who could afford to stay in school or who were articulate and verbally oriented when they came to school in the first place.

But the response of the English teaching profession has not simply been defensive. The past decade has witnessed a dramatic increase in concern for research in the teaching of written composition, drawing on a research base developed in the 1960s through the Federally funded Project English Centers and the National Defense Education Act summer institutes for teachers. It was during the sixties that composition researchers articulated most clearly that "the tradition" in teaching writing—what would now be labeled the "basic skills approach"—was not working. And this discovery was no mere romanticism, though it was closely linked to some sixties phenomena like the "open classroom" and "child centered" movements. But the tradition—teaching children grammar and parts of speech year after year, having them write endless "topic sentences" and standardized practice paragraphs— was not working and could not be shown to have worked in any era of educational history.

The research of the sixties focused on the concept of writing-as-process, rather than writing as a product, based on the assumption that what students need to learn are not the fixed forms of adult language—the traits of "good" writing—but the prewriting, writing, and postwriting processes that must be mastered for a writer to face new writing tasks successfully. The research of that period was sound, it seems to me, and it is unfortunate that the crisis in literacy perceived and popularized by the media in recent years has discredited that approach. Writing-as-process has been widely blamed for a decline in literacy that has not taken place. I wish it were true that the process-centered, child-oriented approach *had* dominated the schools in the seventies, for then we would have a rich body of data to explore. In fact, the tradition in teaching writing was hardly budged, and when people nowadays call for "back to basics," they are, in fact, calling for a return to an approach that has demonstrably proven itself ineffective, the approach which must be perceived as responsible for any lack of writing ability in today's children.

The research of the 1970s has continued to focus on the process approach, building on the foundation constructed in the 1960s. As we look toward improving writing instruction in the 1980s and '90s, it is important that the ideology of the "back to basics" movement not be allowed to cloud issues and to obscure that research base.

I will not, in this paper, attempt to summarize all the research in this area. "Composition theory" is a hot topic on a great many university campuses today, so hot, in fact, that that a number of graduate students are being attracted to it as the sole area in English studies where Ph.D.s are immanently hirable. This, in turn, has produced an avalanche of research studies, most of them sound, but too many to encapsulate in a short paper.[2] Instead, I want to offer, without a great deal of documented "supporting evidence," what I regard as three major "points of agreement" among writing theorists and informed writing teachers today. These form a set of basic, though tentative, premises about the teaching of writing that can be used as the basis for developing sound writing programs today. (As an aside, I want to note that these "points of agreement" are broad enough to include both so-called "basic writers" and writers who have a higher level of skill. I see no need for us to isolate basic writers from other students or to perceive that their needs and learning processes are somehow different from those of their more skilled peers.)

The first area where I find near universal agreement in the profession is that *writing is a learn-by-doing skill*. This notion has not been discovered by researchers of the seventies or sixties, but has been afloat in the profession for over one hundred years. John Dewey knew it and articulated it clearly. So did a minority of school and college English teachers in the nineteenth century. In simplest terms—though not by any means simplistic—it means that drill and exercise neither teach nor prepare a student for writing, that there is no substitute for learning to write through actual writing practice. Now, there is in the profession a great deal of disagreement about what constitutes the best kind of actual practice. Some, for example, suggest that practice should be limited to functional writing forms—essays, application blanks, and so forth—while others, and I am among them, feel that all students should be given a rich variety of writing experiences, including creative as well as functional forms.

But again: *Writing is a learn-by-doing skill*. All the research and theoretical writing of the past two decades points this direction, suggesting that the great need in the schools and colleges today is for more writing, and less, not more, drill in the so-called basics. If *Newsweek* had issued a complaint that Johnny and Jane do not write *enough*, that they write too seldom in English and other classes, that they are too often given drill and short answer tests *in lieu* of actual writing and essay examinations, I would have joined in the outcry. As it is, the back-to-basics movement is actually decreasing the amount of writing students do in the schools, consuming time that could be spent assigning compositions and discussing them by engaging students in yet another round of textbook study largely unrelated to their skills as writers.

A second major point of agreement is that *writing is a liberal art*, and, I am tempted to say, *THE liberal art*. Traditionally, composition has been perceived as a "service skill." One learned to write in order to be able to get down ideas from other subject areas in language. Writing was taught, then, in service to other subjects and disciplines and as an aid to functioning successfully in the world of business.

Recent research, however, has suggested that writing serves far more important functions in education. "Writing," goes a catch phrase in the profession these days, "is a mode of thinking and knowing." Research into the language learning process shows that composition is not merely the jotting down of ideas preformed in the writer's head; the writing process is inextricably bound up with the discovery of knowledge—knowledge of the world and knowledge of one's self—and that the process of writing itself is a process of discovery. "How do I know what I mean until I say it?" is also a popular catch phrase. It can be rephrased to apply to writing as, "How do I know what I know until I write it?"

Writing is more than just a service skill, and attempts to reduce writing instruction to "service" status merely hamper good instruction. Writing is important to the scientist not simply because it allows him to put down his ideas in print, but because it is a part of the discovery process. It is important to the historian, not simply because it allows her to take notes and describe concepts, but because it helps her shape those concepts.

If writing were merely a tool in the service of other disciplines, its skills could probably be taught in a year or less, quite possibly with self-paced computer learning programs. But writing is more than that. As a liberal art it is literally a foundation skill for learning in all disciplines. In claiming a place for writing among the liberal arts, then, writing teachers are not drawing on the old cultural enrichment model, suggesting that writing, like Latin or Greek or humanities study, subtly enriches a person (though it does). They have shown that it is a practical liberal art, absolutely essential to the learning process.

This realization, in turn, suggests that the teaching of writing cannot and should not be exclusively the domain of English teachers, and there is a great deal of interest these days in programs of "writing across the curriculum," in which English and subject-matter teachers deal with those aspects of literacy most directly related to their areas of interest and expertise. (I will have more to say about such programs in my summary and recommendations.)

The third principal point of agreement in the teaching of writing is that *novice writers can (and must) learn to monitor the effectiveness and correctness of their own writing*. The research base to which I referred earlier has rather clearly shown that teachers' written comments on students' writing are not especially effective, even when done thoughtfully and constructively. Students too seldom attend to written comments—even when "forced" to through grading provisions—and there is reason to question whether criticism offered after the act of composition can be effective. Further, the traditional assumption that a teacher must carefully evaluate[3] every piece of writing a student does has created an impossible burden for writing teachers: If they assigned as much writing as experts say they should, they cannot possibly mark it all.

Since the early 1960s, a number of researchers and practitioners have experimented with the related concepts of *peer* and *self-* editing, using pairs and small groups as a way of teaching editorial skills to youngsters and helping them become more and more responsible for the final quality of their own work. This approach is pedagogically justifiable in that it seeks to make writers independent of the English teacher as an arbiter of correctness and strives to develop in the writer a sense of his or her own competence. At the same time, peer- and self-editing demonstrably reduce the take home paper load, substituting class workshops and conferences as a means of teacher evaluation.

This approach to evaluation is still in its infancy, and, predictably, it is both unsettling and troublesome to many teachers. It creates feelings of guilt for some teachers who don't feel as if they are doing their job unless they take home stacks of papers, and there are many, many practical barriers to success, including the use of students who are not highly skilled editors to assist each other in learning. But despite its drawbacks, peer and self-editing is one of the most promising practices in the teaching of writing today, and I am quite confident that further research and practical experimentation will make it a permanent part of writing pedagogy, if only because it allows writing teachers to assign vastly more amounts of writing than they were able to formerly.

Having identified three major points of agreement within the writing profession, I now want to turn to some matters that are less settled—some points of disagreement among writing teachers and some persisting problems that come from outside the profession.

For example, there is a persisting problem of what I consider the demeaning of composition and composition teachers. Both within and outside English, composition is seen as dirty work, a necessary evil. Subject matter teachers in both school and college are quick to dump the burden of teaching writing on basic English courses and are generally unwilling to deal with problems of literacy in their own classes. Composition classes are frequently staffed by "part-timers" at the college level and by the newest teachers in the schools, the latter a sure sign that the older, experienced teachers regard the teaching of literature as more important. At the college level again, writing teachers and specialists are not rewarded or promoted as quickly as literature teachers, an attitude on the part of collegians that has been passed on to generations of school teachers.

The national concern for literacy and basic skills instruction of the past decade clearly implies that attitudes toward composition and composition teachers ought to change. Undergraduate and graduate programs are producing a new breed of English teachers, a teacher who is often well informed about writing theory and sees the teaching of writing as valuable and important. Such teachers need to be recruited vigorously, hired, and rewarded for their work. Those teachers in the schools who have demonstrated interest in writing instruction already should likewise be rewarded and their commitment acknowledged. The hiring of "temporaries" and part-timers and the use of teachers who have only minored in English or who have no significant amount of training in language and composition must come to an end.

The use of non-specialists and the demeaning of writing teachers is a very old problem. A newer one, and a pernicious one, is the confusion of *testing* with *teaching*, and I am referring here to the current epidemic of state, local, and national testing programs that has spread across the country in the past decade. In one school system after another, educational leaders have reached the conclusion that instituting a testing program and collecting data on students' verbal skills will create pressure for teachers to do a better job with writing instruction. I would not recommend the total elimination of sound, theoretically consistent assessment programs as a source of useful data for teachers and parents. But at the present time, testing is beginning to substitute for teaching. Reasonably enough, teachers teach to the tests, and in many schools and school districts, the only actual writing instruction being done is in preparation for examinations. The net effect of many testing programs has been to blunt the direction of the learn-to-write-by-writing movement. Test scores may rise, but there is no substantial evidence that students' global literacy, their ability to use language in non-test situations is increased.

The testing phenomenon is one that has, for the most part, come from outside the English teaching profession, and it has been acquiesced to only with great reluctance. English teachers generally know that testing is not teaching. But a third problem area is one that is clearly an internal matter for the profession, and that is the persistence of drill, rote work, and isolated basic skill instruction in the face of voluminous research which shows the near valuelessness of such practices.[4]

In simplest terms, we English teachers cling to *grammar*—tenaciously, nostalgically, stubbornly. "Grammar" books, by which I mean standard handbooks of grammar and usage, are selling better than ever these days, and it is English teachers, for the most part, who are responsible for the wholesale adoption and use of these obsolete texts. Now if you believe what you read in *Newsweek* and the popular press, and if you take at face value what the public says it wants, you would think that the persistence of grammar books simply shows that English teachers are being responsible educators. And there is no question that despite some changes in methodology, in most school districts, *the public is getting exactly what it wants*: more "basics," more drill.

But as I have already shown, in the end, more "basics" is not what is needed in the schools. What is needed is more writing—with due attention paid to matters of form and correctness—not a wholesale return to the sentence diagram. English teachers ought to know better than to go back to the grammar books, and they ought to be putting up more resistance before succumbing to public pressure for simplistic "writing" programs that do not teach writing at all.

The persistence of grammar and drill is understandable, given public pressures, and good writing teachers need the support of enlightened school administrators who know that writing is learned by writing, not by dissecting textbook sentences or by correcting errors in somebody else's paragraph. At the same time, it is a matter of great concern to those of us involved with professional organizations like the National Council of Teachers of English that the word on grammar and skill drill has not gotten into a great many classrooms in this country.

Summary and Recommendations

Although there are points of disagreement and inconsistency within the English teaching community, and despite external pressures which, in many cases, are inconsistent with language learning theory and research, I think it is safe to say in broad summary that the time is right for dramatic change in writing instruction. The schools are staffed by hundreds of thousands of teachers who are unhappy about the way they teach Johnny and Jane to write. Equally concerned are millions of parents and school administrators, not to mention students themselves, who are often acutely aware of their own writing deficiencies. The will to change exists. So do the resources, for that matter, because teaching writing is remarkably inexpensive, requiring pens, paper, and willing teachers, not a massive infusion of new funds for electronic hardware and laboratories. I believe this change can be accomplished if the public, administrators, and English teachers can set four imperatives as the guidelines for program development.

1. *Writing programs must be based on frequent, authentic writing experiences, for all students—basic or advanced—and with a corresponding decrease in isolated drill in so-called language basic skills.* The question for the 1980s is *not* whether Johnny and Jane have mastered mandated objectives or hierarchical patterns of

discreet language skills, but how often they write, to whom, for what purposes, and under what kind of professional guidance.

2. *Writing-across-the-curriculum projects must be developed by English and other subject matter faculty and put into place so that writing is used in all classes, not just English/language arts classes.* The implications of this recommendation are broad and complex, the subject for another paper,[5] but I find in my work in the schools that there is great interest in it, both among English teachers and subject area teachers. I believe it is possible *now* for schools to develop comprehensive programs in which writing is a part of every classroom and English and subject teachers agree on a division of labor (and satisfaction) that uses writing to enhance learning in all areas.

3. *Inservice and staff development for English and content area teachers must be expanded, preferably at the expense of testing programs.* The success of the National Writing Project, an inservice program funded by the National Endowment for the Humanities that operates in almost every state, shows that the way to improve writing instruction in the schools is to help teachers educate themselves about current methodology, not to threaten them with standardized tests. Inservice is expensive, of course, but it can be effective, and if the money currently being channeled into testing programs were redirected toward well-conceived inservice, there would be plenty of funds to reeducate all willing teachers with some left over for modest and equally well-conceived evaluation and assessment programs.

4. *Composition teachers must be given more satisfactory teaching conditions, including manageable class sizes and loads.* For over two decades the National Council of Teachers of English has advocated class loads for secondary English teachers not to exceed one hundred students and four classes. But during those decades we have seen class sizes and loads in most states increase, not decrease. Even drawing on contemporary peer-editing techniques, no teacher can be fully effective teaching writing to massive numbers of students. If schools are serious about wanting to improve writing instruction, they might well begin by assessing the composition load being given their teachers and making certain those loads are in keeping with the NCTE recommendations.

I have suggested that the will to change and improve writing instruction exists. So, I believe, does the know-how. Informed English teachers *do* know how to get the Johnnys and Janes writing and growing as writers. English teachers can, working with fellow faculty, with parents, and with administrators, develop sound and assessable programs that produce competent writers. The problem facing those of us concerned about writing instruction in the schools is to find an outlet for that good will and know-how so that by the end of the decade the schools will have moved forward to an age of heightened literacy, not further back into the dark ages of basic skill instruction.

NOTES

1. See, for example, *The English Journal,* "Why Johnny Can't Write," January 1976, for several analyses of the issues.
2. For more detailed and comprehensive research summaries, see Charles Cooper and Lee Odell, eds. *Evaluating Writing* (Urbana, Ill.: National Council of Teachers of English, 1977) and Stephen Judy and Susan Judy, *An Introduction to Teaching Writing* (New York: John Wiley, 1981).
3. Please note the word *evaluate* in this sentence. In this context, it means "read and write critical comments" on a paper. Contemporary writing theory seriously questions whether this sort of evaluation is effective, but in general, theorists and practitioners are still agreed that teachers ought to read everything the student writes (at some point in the composition process) and respond to it.
4. Probably the single best summary of this research is Elizabeth Haynes, "Using Research in Preparing to Teach Writing." *The English Journal* 67 (January 1978), 82-88.
5. See, for example, my *ABC's of Literacy* (New York: Oxford, 1980), for a book-length discussion of interdisciplinary reading and writing programs.

A TEACHER LOOKS AT WRITING

Beverly J. Bimes
The Lindenwood College

Looking at the stacks of ungraded papers, the exhausted teacher wonders why she bothers teaching writing to students who never feel the slightest need to write. With the haunting evidence of her failure before her, she turns to the chore of grading papers written by unwilling writers and vows that it will be a long time before she asks them to write again.

It is easy to share this teacher's frustration, for hers is not an isolated case; teaching writing has become a source of frustration for both teachers and students. Although there is no "quick fix" to ensure the development of competent, willing writers, there is hope for the beleaguered teacher. Through such projects as the National Writing Project and through extensive writing research, much theory and information is now available to help teachers develop successful writing programs. A new approach to teaching writing has emerged.

The Writing Environment

In this new approach the teacher's attitude toward writing is vital. What he or she does in the classroom—in creating an atmosphere for writing—can determine whether or not a student even attempts to write. If students are asked to write in an environment which is threatening, unpleasant, and dictatorial, they will seldom become fluent writers. A study by Donald Graves (1973) reveals that an informal classroom encourages more student writing. Cooper (1976) cites the importance of having high expectations and a positive attitude in producing student writers, while Phillip Lopate (1978) notes the importance of creating the proper environment for writing. These researchers support the premise that an atmosphere which encourages writers to feel secure, to take risks, and to collaborate with each other is essential.

In setting the stage for writing, teachers must investigate their perceptions of themselves as writing teachers. The teacher who can exchange a judgmental, dogmatic role for the role of an editor is more successful in helping reluctant writers achieve success. As a result of this exchange, all writing is placed on a continuum; the teacher-editor advances each student along this continuum. At the end of the year, each student may not be a perfect writer, but he will be a better writer. To facilitate this view of writing, to move beyond the role of being a mere critic, teachers must become writers themselves. The works of Donald Murray (1978) and Donald Graves (1978) stress the importance of the teacher as a writer. In becoming a writer, the teacher gains valuable insights about the nature of assignments. When teachers understand the importance of creating an atmosphere for writing and becoming editors rather than critics, they encourage students and build confidence in themselves and in those they teach.

Purpose and Audience

The development of writing abilities also depends on the kinds of writing students are asked to do and the various audiences for whom they write. Students are often given assignments with no real purpose or audience. As a result, the writing is often meaningless, for students feel neither the desire nor the need to write. Arthur Applebee and his associates at Stanford University monitored more than 1,000 teachers in various disciplines, asking them to describe the writing tasks they assign.

Applebee (1981) reported that most writing tasks required students to fill in information, to translate, to do worksheets, and to take multiple choice tests. Some assignments even involved copying sections of a textbook. Applebee found that the majority of writing assignments in schools were designed for assessment—to see if students had learned. Very few assignments actually helped students become better writers. Donald Murray (1978) speaks of the importance of moving beyond the use of writing for assessment, arguing that the most significant step in teaching composition comes when students discover meaning through writing and use language as a tool to move beyond what they already know.

Too often, students never have the chance to do this sort of writing, partly because teachers lack the training to teach writing effectively. Unfortunately, courses in the teaching of writing did not exist in colleges until recently. Hence, teachers are often unaware of the various purposes or functions of writing and the kinds of audiences that students should address. For these teachers, James Britton's work (1975) on categorizing the purposes and audiences of writing is helpful, offering them a means to design significant writing assignments. By dividing the purposes of writing into three categories—expressive, transactive, and poetic—Britton provides a model for composition teachers.

When teachers understand that expressive writing—writing in which students express their feelings, attitudes, and ideas—is fundamental to developing mature, textured writing, they are more likely to construct assignments that allow students to discover knowledge rather than to regurgitate what has already been learned. All writing begins from within. As students are awakened to their own perceptions, they are better able to articulate more of their world in language. Unfortunately, much writing in school is limited to the unexpressive transactional mode. Researchers in one project found that the demand for impersonal, unexpressive writing actively inhibits learning (Martin, et al., 1976).

In addition to understanding the purposes of writing, teachers should consider the various audiences which students need to address. In school, students write almost exclusively for an evaluating teacher; as a result, their work often has little vitality because it lacks a sense of genuineness—a sense of reality. Seldom in life do adults write to someone who already knows more than they do about a subject, someone who will then evaluate how well they write. Yet this kind of judgmental audience is the only one many students will ever experience.

Teachers need to become more aware of the various types of audiences for which students can write. Here, for example, are some audiences identified by Martin et al. and based on Britton's work: child (or adolescent) to self; child (or adolescent) to trusted adult; pupil to teacher as partner in dialogue; pupil to teacher seen as examiner or assessor; child (or adolescent) to peer (as expert, co-worker, friend, etc.); and writer to his readers (or unknown audience). Developing a sense of audience is basic to developing writing abilities. When students identify audience, they recognize the need for different organization patterns, word choices, and styles. They consider the reader, and their writing becomes writing to be read. Writing thus becomes more purposeful, and the writer experiences satisfaction with what he or she has written.

In evaluating a recent writing workshop, one participant commented as follows:

> I am forty-four years old, and this is the first time I have written for pleasure since I was a senior in high school. At that time, a teacher read aloud and ridiculed before the class a paper I had written. From that time on, I wrote only when it was an assignment; writing was something I went to great ends to avoid. But today I wrote for my peers. They selected my writing as the best of the group. I even won a blue ribbon! I have a lot of writing to catch up on!

What could be a more enthusiastic endorsement for broadening the audiences of young writers?

The Writing Process

For more than a decade, researchers and educators have viewed writing as a process involving prewriting, composing, and editing (Britton, 1978; Elbow, 1973; Graves, 1975, 1978; Murray, 1973). At every stage of this process, students should have full access to the resources necesary to help them succeed. They should be assured that it is acceptable to take risks and to use their knowledge of language as a basis for writing. The process approach suggests that writing is developmental and that writers go through several stages in producing a written work. From the work of Flower and Hayes (1980), it is clear that these stages are not always separate or linear in nature. Nevertheless, identification of the stages of the writing process makes the teaching of writing easier.

Prewriting includes experiences that help students feel, see, assess, synthesize, and discover that they have something to say on a particular topic. It is a time of incubation that should encourage the generation of information, concepts, and generalizations; the limitation of the topic; the development of a controlling idea; the identification of audience and purpose; and the establishment of an atmosphere wherein students feel free to think and write. Pre-writing includes a variety of teaching techniques: speaking, listening, conversing, discussing, role-playing, reading aloud, reciting, and brainstorming. And even writing itself can function as a pre-writing activity, with free writing, journal writing, and the written interview serving as springboards to more formal types of writing. Pre-writing is essential to successful writing, for it helps students feel self-confident enough to express their attitudes and ideas to others.

In the *composing* stage writers translate their ideas into words. Teachers can help students prior to this stage by teaching specific language skills to help them successfully complete assignments. These skills, however, should be taught in context rather than through isolated exercises. Emphasizing skills at a time when students know they are going to use them immediately is an effective way to help writers. Britton believes the teacher is important in creating a desire to write, in giving students ways to attack new problems and absorb difficult information. Students often fail to complete writing assignments simply because they do not understand what is expected of them or because they believe they lack the necessary skills.

Modeling is one technique that can be used early in the composing stage. The teacher should use several different kinds of models, including student models, before having students attempt original work. Showing is better than telling, and models can inspire confidence by showing students that their peers have written successfully.

Revising and editing are important steps in the writing process. Revising is the reworking of ideas to assure that the writer's intended meaning is communicated, and editing is the refinement and correction of the mechanics of the paper. Both these skills can be taught effectively when students share their writing with one another and talk about it (Elbow, 1973). Peer teaching and peer editing become integral parts of the writing process and create enthusiasm for writing. A fringe benefit of this collaborative endeavor is its effect on the classroom, for it creates a community of learners, where students are involved in writing, not as mere spectators, but as a vital part of the learning process.

When students and teachers view writing as a process, students are more willing to write because they feel free to experiment, to ask for help, to express their feelings honestly, and to share their writing. In essence, they have discovered writing.

Teachers also discover that writing is not a mystical art; it *can* be taught effectively. By understanding the process, they can help students become hooked on writing.

This approach to writing instruction—the creation of a positive teacher attitude and a non-threatening atmosphere, the identification of audience and purpose, and the viewing of writing as a process—can almost guarantee success in improving student writers; however, many students will never be exposed to writing in this way, for teachers of writing are now engaged in a battle—a battle between cherished myths about how students learn to write and the reality of how they actually develop abilities. It has become a battle of forced choices—"You're either with us or against us!"

The Role of Grammar

The rallying cry of the back-to-basics advocates is "Teach them grammar; grammar is the secret to writing well." Writing researchers and those involved in programs such as the National Writing Project arm themselves for battle with research showing that the study of grammar in a "drill me-skill me" fashion has no direct effect on the development of writing ability (Britton, 1970; Hoyt, 1906; Lyman, 1921; Pooley, 1958). Enemy camps form; emotions run rampant; and, unfortunately, the real issue is lost. The question is not *whether* to teach grammar, but rather *how* to teach it.

Researchers agree that young writers need to encounter writing situations which allow them to work on their language. They should learn the principles of grammar and good usage by using language, not by being exposed to isolated exercises in grammar. Sentence combining can be one way to provide students with an integrated approach to learning the structure of the language through writing. Daiker, Kerek, and Morenberg (1979) report that sentence combining produces growth in the syntactic maturity of students' sentences, improves overall writing ability, and creates positive attitudes toward revision. In teaching the student how to manipulate language through sentence combining, the teacher instills an awareness of the stylistic options available in sentence construction.

Structure and Sequence

Another issue in the battle over how to teach writing concerns structure and sequence. Although it is essential that students learn skills, it is difficult to say precisely when they should do so. In a thirteen-year study of language development K-12, Walter Loban (1976) reports that charts of sequence and stages might inhibit learning for children who vary tremendously in language ability. Students are often much more capable at every level than they are perceived to be. Graves' observations (1977) of children's writing behavior and his analysis of their products support this premise.

Consider the energetic sixth-grader who announces that she is going to write a novel. Her teacher tries to discourage her by saying, "A novel? Why not write a short story? Start with a smaller, more approachable task." But in talking with her, the teacher finds that the student has an experience to share—a summer on a dude ranch, where she saw a miniature range war. Despite the discouraging words from the teacher, the student successfully completes a short novel, illustrates it, and entitles it *The Western Duel*. Later, the same student enters an essay contest without telling anyone. When the teacher receives notification that the student has won, she is surprised. The student responds, "Once you've written a novel, you can do anything!"

As an eighth grader, this same student despises writing. Why? The curriculum guide states that all eighth graders will be able to write a good paragraph. As a

26

result, all of the writing assignments in her class are limited to paragraph writing. Does it make sense to limit a successful novelist and award-winning essay writer to writing paragraphs?

The danger of overemphasizing sequence and structure is that a lockstep approach to composition emerges. When all assignments reflect a rigid adherence to a specific structure, students are locked in to our feeble expectations and are not allowed to discover what they can do in writing.

A New Approach to Writing

Perhaps the time wasted in battling over how writing should be taught is near an end due to the efforts of those associated with the National Writing Project. Through their efforts, many of the myths about the teaching of writing are being dispelled. In the past, educators have had difficulty in seeing that research filtered down to its appropriate audience—teachers and students; seldom has research resulted in practical application, the improvement of instruction and learning. But more recently, in eighty-five writing projects across the country, teachers are being exposed to the latest research and theory about writing, are learning to translate this theory into workable classroom strategies, are becoming writers themselves, and are learning how to return to their districts and give in-service training to other teachers. When teachers teach teachers, there is no credibility gap, no condemnation or division into enemy camps. The approach is practical and simple: "I have some information to share which will help your students become better writers and which will help you feel more confident in the teaching of writing."

This new approach to the teaching of writing enables teachers to have a keen sense of direction and confidence in developing writing programs. As previously discussed in this paper, the most significant aspects of this approach are as follows:

1. The attitude of the teacher.
2. The proper environment for writing—a non-threatening environment where students feel free to take risks.
3. The identification of audience and purpose in writing and the structuring of assignments so that students are given the opportunity to write for a variety of audiences and purposes.
4. The viewing of writing as a process, including the stages of prewriting, composing, and editing.
5. The teaching of grammar by integrating it into the writing process through such activities as sentence combining.
6. The avoidance of a lock-step approach to sequence and structure.

Recommendations

It is imperative that a continuous effort be made to educate teachers on how students really learn to write. Instruction in writing must go beyond the English classroom and extend to all teachers. Writing is a vital skill in every discipline, and all teachers need to be encouraged to teach writing. Writing projects are an excellent way of providing training for teachers. Administrators also need to know the research about writing so that they can support teachers and provide leadership in developing and implementing significant writing programs.

Equally important is educating an uninformed public. If teachers hope to have an impact on young writers, they need the support and help of a broader society. Parents are a key to this kind of support. By giving workshops for parents which show how they can become involved in the teaching of writing, teachers will gain support and, in addition, children will receive the message that their parents value writing.

Teachers also need to seek support from business and government. Too often, children get mixed messages about the importance of writing in a media-dominated society. It is difficult for them to become enthusiastic over a skill which appears to lack value in the real world. To assure students that writing is, indeed, a life skill, programs should be developed which allow interaction between successful adults—from the corporate and civic sectors—and students. These adults would describe practical, job-related writing skills to students and show that writing is an important part of their world. With financial cutbacks threatening the very existence of many fine writing programs, this new relationship between industry and schools might provide the incentive for needed financial assistance to ensure survival of these programs.

If students are to become better writers, we must inform educators and the public about how writing abilities develop and make them partners in the teaching of writing. If we redirect our energies toward this goal, we will no longer waste time engaged in a senseless, rhetorical battle. The result will be the development of eager, willing writers and enthusiastic, confident teachers of writing. Could there be a better victory?

REFERENCES

Applebee, Arthur. *Writing in the Secondary School: English and the Content Areas*. Urbana: NCTE, 1981.

Britton, James. "Now That You Go to School." In *Children and Writing in the Elementary School: Theories and Techniques*. Richard L. Larson, ed. New York: Oxford University Press, 1975.

Britton, James. "The Composing Processes and the Functions of Writing." In *Research on Composing: Points of Departure*. Charles R. Cooper and Lee Odell, eds. Urbana: NCTE, 1978.

Britton, James. "The Student's Writing." *Explorations in Children's Writing*. Eldonna L. Evertts, ed. Urbana: NCTE, 1970.

Cooper, Charles R., et al. "Tonawanda Middle School's New Writing Program." *English Journal*, 1976, Vol. 65, pp. 56-61.

Daiker, Donald A., Kerek, Andrew, and Morenberg, Max, eds. *Sentence Combining and the Teaching of Writing*. Conway, AR: L&S Books, 1979.

Elbow, Peter. *Writing without Teachers*. New York: Oxford University Press, 1973.

Flower, Linda, and Hayes, Jack. "Cognitive-Process Theory of Writing." Paper presented at the Conference on College Composition and Communication, Washington, D.C., March, 1980.

Graves, Donald H. "An Examination of the Writing Processes of Seven-Year-Old Children." *Research in the Teaching of English*, 1975, 9, pp. 227-41.

Graves, Donald H. *Balance the Basics: Let Them Write*. New York: The Ford Foundation, 1978.

Graves, Donald H. "Children's Writing: Research Directions and Hypotheses Based Upon an Examination of the Writing Processes of Seven-Year-Olds." Ph.D. dissertation, State University of New York at Buffalo, 1973.

Graves, Donald H. "Language Arts Textbooks: A Writing Process Evaluation." *Language Arts*, 1977, Vol. 54, pp. 817-823.

Hoyt, F. S. "The Place of Grammar in the Elementary Curriculum." *Teacher's College Record* of Columbia University, November, 1906.

Lopate, Phillip. "Helping Young Children Start to Write." In *Research on Composing: Points of Departure*. Charles R. Cooper and Lee Odell, eds. Urbana: NCTE, 1978.

Lyman, R. L. "English Grammar in American Schools Before 1850." Bulletin. Department of the Interior, Bureau of Education, 1921.

Martin, Nancy, et al. *Writing and Learning Across the Curriculum 11-16*. London: University of London Institute of Education, 1976.

Murray, Donald M. "The Writing Process." In *Classroom Practices in Teaching English, 1973-74: Language Activities*. Allen Berger and Blanch Hope Smith, co-chairpersons. Urbana: NCTE, 1973.

Murray, Donald M. "Internal Revision: A Process of Discovery." In *Research on Composing: Points of Departure*. Charles R. Cooper and Lee Odell, eds. Urbana: NCTE, 1978.

Pooley, R. C. "What Grammar Shall I Teach?" *English Journal*, 1958, Vol. 47, pp. 327-333.

PART III:
MATHEMATICS

THE BASICS OF MATHEMATICS IN THE EIGHTIES

Shirley Frye
Scottsdale Public Schools

Mathematics educators have taken a stand. No longer will we allow our subject to be limited to the learning of computation as the only basic skill. Instead, applications, measurement, geometry, estimation, problem solving, and functional rules of mathematics will be integral parts of the discipline.

Early in 1976, the National Council of Supervisors of Mathematics (NCSM) responded to challenges of the National Institute of Education and the Euclid Conference on Basic Mathematical Skills and Learning to adopt basic skills as a major priority. The response was a *Position Paper on Basic Mathematical Skills* proclaiming that the narrow view of mathematics as computation was not adequate for our students, the future citizens. These are the Ten Basic Skill Areas defined in the *Position Paper*:

1. Problem Solving

Learning to solve problems is the principal reason for studying mathematics. Problem solving is the process of applying previously acquired knowledge to new and unfamiliar situations. Solving word problems in texts is one form of problem solving, but students also should be faced with non-textbook problems. Problem-solving strategies involve posing questions, analyzing situations, translating results, illustrating results, drawing diagrams, and using trial and error. In solving problems, students need to be able to apply the rules of logic necessary to arrive at valid conclusions. They must be able to determine which facts are relevant. They should also be unafraid of arriving at tentative conclusions and must be willing to subject these conclusions to scrutiny.

2. Applying Mathematics to Everyday Situations

The use of mathematics is interrelated with all computation activities. Students should be encouraged to take everyday situations, translate them into mathematical expressions, solve the mathematics, and interpret the results in light of the initial situation.

3. Alertness to the Reasonableness of Results

Due to arithmetic or other mistakes, results of mathematical work are sometimes wrong. Students should learn to inspect all results and to check for reasonableness in terms of the original problem. With the increase in the use of calculating devices, this skill is essential.

4. Estimation and Approximation

Students should be able to carry out rapid approximate calculations by first rounding off numbers. They should acquire some simple techniques for estimating quantity, length, distance, weight, etc., and should be able to decide when a particular result is precise enough for the purpose at hand.

5. Appropriate Computational Skills

Students should gain facility with addition, subtraction, multiplication, and division with whole numbers and decimals. Today it must be recognized that long, complicated computations will usually be done with a calculator. But knowledge of single-digit number facts is essential, and mental arithmetic is still a valuable skill. Moreover, there are everyday situations which demand recognition of, and simple computation with, common fractions. Because consumers continually deal with many situations that involve percentage, the ability to recognize and use percents should also be developed and maintained.

6. Geometry

Students should learn the geometric concepts they will need to function effectively in the three-dimensional world. They should have knowledge of concepts such as point, line, plane, parallel, and perpendicular. They should know basic properties of simple geometric figures, particularly those properties which relate to measurement and problem-solving skills. They also must be able to recognize similarities and differences among objects.

7. Measurement

As a minimum skill, students should be able to measure distance, weight, time, capacity, and temperature. Measurements of angles and calculations of simple areas and volumes are also essential. Students should be able to perform measurement in both metric and customary systems using the appropriate tools.

8. Reading, Interpreting, And Constructing Tables, Charts, and Graphs

Students should know how to read and draw conclusions from simple tables, maps, charts, and graphs. They should be able to condense numerical information into more manageable or meaningful terms by setting up simple tables, charts and graphs.

9. Using Mathematics To Predict

Students should learn how elementary notions of probability are used to determine the likelihood of future events. They should learn to identify situations where immediate past experience does not affect the likelihood of future events. They should become familiar with how mathematics is used to help make predictions such as election forecasts.

10. Computer Literacy

It is important for all citizens to understand what computers can and cannot do. Students should be aware of their use in teaching/learning, financial transactions, and information storage and retrieval. The "mystique" surrounding computers is disturbing and can put persons with no understanding of computers at a disadvantage. The increasing use of computers by government, industry, and business demands an awareness of computer uses and limitations.

The following chart (adapted from the NCSM's *Position Paper*) illustrates the expected outcomes associated with various levels of skills, suggesting that employment opportunities may well depend on the kinds of skills learned.

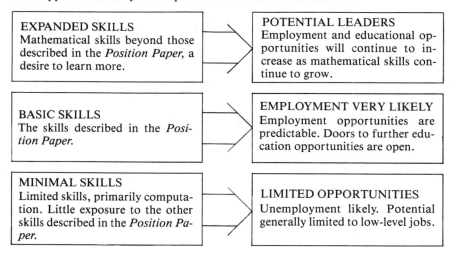

EXPANDED SKILLS
Mathematical skills beyond those described in the *Position Paper*, a desire to learn more.

POTENTIAL LEADERS
Employment and educational opportunities will continue to increase as mathematical skills continue to grow.

BASIC SKILLS
The skills described in the *Position Paper*.

EMPLOYMENT VERY LIKELY
Employment opportunities are predictable. Doors to further education opportunities are open.

MINIMAL SKILLS
Limited skills, primarily computation. Little exposure to the other skills described in the *Position Paper*.

LIMITED OPPORTUNITIES
Unemployment likely. Potential generally limited to low-level jobs.

The impact of the *Position Paper* has far exceeded the NCSM's expectations. Teachers, administrators, school boards, colleges of education, and authors of textbooks have listened to the premises and have adopted the NCSM's comprehensive, reasonable list as a definition of basic mathematics skills.

The National Council of Teachers of Mathematics (NCTM), as an organization of professional educators, felt a special obligation to present responsible directions for mathematics programs in the 1980s. At its annual meeting in Seattle, April 1980, the Council publicly took a forthright stand in its document, *An Agenda for Action: Recommendation for School Mathematics in the 1980s*. In summary, the NCTM recommends that

(1) problem solving be the focus of school mathematics in the 1980s;
(2) basic skills in mathematics be defined to encompass more than computational facility;
(3) mathematics programs take full advantage of the power of calculators and computers at all grade levels;
(4) stringent standards of both effectiveness and efficiency be applied to the teaching of mathematics;
(5) the success of mathematics programs and student learning be evaluated by a wider range of measures than conventional testing;
(6) more mathematics study be required for all students and a flexible curriculum with a greater range of options be designed to accommodate the diverse needs of the student population;
(7) mathematics teachers demand of themselves and their colleagues a high level of professionalism;
(8) public support for mathematics instruction be raised to a level commensurate with the importance of mathematical understanding to individuals and society.

In an effort to provide the youth of our country with the best mathematics education, knowledgeable educators from NCSM and NCTM have assumed the leadership in giving directions to mathematics programs and for mathematics teachers.

The expanded definition of basic skills and new goals for mathematics will require teachers to transfer computation skills to applications and to problem solving strategies. The use of mathematics will increase and change with the challenges of space exploration, economic complexity, micro-electronics, and discoveries in other fields. As we are able to perceive it on the basis of today's technology alone, the future will be drastically different. Methods that were successful in the past may not work in the future, education will not be a function of school alone, and the emphasis will be on a lifelong learning of skills.

In the past, man focused on solving problems of the world as it existed. Now and in the future, society will focus on problems in the world as humans have shaped it. Dennis Avery in his article "Futuristic Education" (*Education Leadership*, February 1980), advises us that the problems of tomorrow will require new skills, including a tolerance for multiple interpretations and the ability to explore and to create alternatives. In the 1980s and 1990s there will be, according to Avery, a need to "redefine knowledge, schooling, and education. The emphasis will be on learning how to learn, rather than on learning facts. Learning will move from a knowing to a searching emphasis."

Certainly this new emphasis suggests that teachers of the 1980s will need instructional alternatives and new techniques. We will also need to revise curricular goals and provide for ongoing inservice by school districts, support for educational change by parents and legislators, and a willingness by individual teachers to change and grow.

In elementary schools, the transfer of skills to applications must be carefully planned, with problem solving treated as a specific strand in the curriculum and developed at every level. Problem solving encompasses much more than "word" or "story" problems in textbooks, for it allows students to use alternative methods to find solutions. The *Agenda for Action* notes that "researchers and funding agencies should give priority to investigation into the nature of problem solving and to effective ways to develop problem solvers." Support should be provided for the following:

— analysis of effective strategies
— the identification of effective techniques for teaching
— new programs aimed at preparing teachers for teaching problem solving skills
— investigation of attitudes related to problem solving skills
— the development of good prototype material for teaching the skills of problem solving, using all media

In high schools, mathematics teachers can no longer assume that students learn consumer skills by observation or some mysterious method. Rather, all students need formal experience in learning and practicing the important mathematics skills needed by the wise consumer. In grades 7-9 the minimal exposure to consumer applications is insufficient to equip all students for the complicated economic and monetary decision of adulthood. In my own district in Scottsdale, Arizona, students are required to enroll in one semester of Consumer Mathematics in their senior year. Teachers have discovered that the majority of students do need and benefit from a specific course in consumer mathematics as well as from an exit experience to review and maintain previously learned skills.

The senior year is an especially good time for the requirement since seniors have the maturity to realize the value of the material, the motivation for becoming independent, and the anticipation of becoming taxpayers. In the classes, every effort is made to ensure a positive final experience in mathematics so that students leave school confident in their ability to apply mathematics to their consumer needs. Group work and calculators help provide a successful experience for all students.

Motivating and encouraging students are two ways to maintain their interest in continuing study. For example, relating mathematics to the various skills needed for careers convinces them that studying will indeed pay off in future work. Since the transfer of school skills to application does not occur automatically, teachers must be aware of the many career applications of mathematics, and they must present topics in the context of these applications. The teacher unlocks the door to the uses of mathematics in the out-of-school world, and educators must meet the challenge of anticipating for their students the careers of the next century.

One of the recommendations of the NCTM is that at least three years of mathematics be required in grades 9-12. This should encourage schools to devise flexible curricula to accommodate the diverse needs of students. Also, it demands that teachers utilize creative methods to provide success in mathematics for all students. No longer can the attrition rate in mathematics courses be a point of pride. We must develop programs to hold students, programs that do not require every student to learn the same content and to develop the same skills. Steps should be taken to assure that all students gain a foundation in mathematics essential to fulfilling their potential as productive citizens.

If education purports to equip students to cope with their surroundings, then learning to use calculators and computers is an important part of basic skills. The pervasive use of calculators and computers today is justification enough for including these valuable learning tools in our schools. Initially, teachers need a general working knowledge of calculators and computers if they are to be used effectively for learning concepts and solving problems. In a cogent article, Stuart Milnar advises that "Educators can no longer ignore the implications of the microcomputer revolution. Only a few years ago most educators felt that the role of computers in education would be defined sometime in the future. Microcomputers changed all that—the future is now!" ("Teaching Teachers about Computers: A Necessity for Education," *Phi Delta Kappan*, April 1980, pp. 544-546).

The various NCTM and NCSM recommendations point clearly to a continuing need for dynamic teachers who are constant learners, who do not insulate themselves from the changes in education and the real world. The responsive teacher of the 80s must look at learning theories, teaching methods, and the population to be taught—and be ready to adapt.

Regardless of the hardware involved, the organization used, or the content emphasized, teachers do finally account for student achievement. For this reason, inservice opportunities must be available to keep the teacher refreshed, motivated and prepared for the work of the 1980s.

The special efforts by NCTM and NCSM to set mathematics goals for the 1980s attest to the value of mathematics competence as a social resource. Since the responsibility for that resource is shared by many people, I want to conclude with these recommendations:

TO MATHEMATICS EDUCATORS
— continue to be learners and role models for your students
— be dynamic, caring, and enthusiastic teachers
— improve and update your teaching skills with equipment and technology
— teach a comprehensive program of "basic skills"
— emphasize excellence

TO PARENTS
— support the classroom teacher and the educational system
— demand quality programs that do more than teach rote computation
— rely on the good judgment and expertise of the professional educator
— become informed and involved

TO ADMINISTRATORS AND SCHOOL BOARDS
— give appropriate attention and status to the learning of mathematics
— support the requests for increasing mathematics requirements and for incorporating calculators and computers in the classroom
— provide inservice that relates to content and to local needs
— budget for remuneration that will attract and retain quality teachers
— accept the broad definitions of basic skills

Burn-out, mathematics teacher shortages, math anxiety, and declining enrollments are issues often highlighted today, but in this conference educational leaders are addressing a more critical issue in the curriculum—the basics. I believe that mathematical competency is essential for full participation of our students in tomorrow's world. I hope you find my recommendations for basic mathematics skills realistic and responsible for the decade of the 1980s.

MOVING FORWARD IN MATHEMATICS

Ross Taylor
Minneapolis Public Schools

I. PRESENT AND FUTURE NEEDS

What Basic Mathematics Skills Will All Citizens Need?

As we prepare our students for the 1980s and beyond, we cannot afford to go back to the basics that were needed when books were balanced by men with quill pens sitting on tall stools. In the age of electronic computing we must look forward to the basic skills our students will need as adults. In the past the emphasis has been on facility with paper-and-pencil computational skills. Today, however, with the accessibility of inexpensive calculators and the increasing availability of computers, more and more computation is being done electronically. Therefore, a change in emphasis is in order. Mathematics educators generally agree that basic mathematical skills should include at least the ten basic skill areas identified in the National Council of Supervisors of Mathematics Position Paper on Basic Mathematical Skills[1]:

- Problem Solving
- Applying Mathematics to Everyday Situations
- Alertness to Reasonableness of Results
- Estimation and Approximation
- Appropriate Computational Skills
- Geometry
- Measurement
- Tables, Charts and Graphs
- Using Mathematics to Predict
- Computer Literacy

In its publication *An Agenda for Action: Recommendations for School Mathematics of the 1980s* the National Council of Teachers of Mathematics supports this broad view of basic mathematical skills and stresses that problem solving should be the focus of school mathematics in the 1980s.[2] With the emphasis on problem solving, skills such as estimation and approximation and alertness to reasonableness of results take on increased importance. Computation is still important, but the emphasis is changing. Today and in the future long cumbersome computations will be done electronically, but the ability to do rapid accurate mental computation is more important than ever. Computer literacy is a vital basic skill for the future. All citizens will need to be able to use computers without anxiety and know both the power and the limitations of computers.

What Is Needed Beyond the Basics?

In our increasingly complex technological society a strong background in mathematics is becoming essential. Students need to know that the amount and type of mathematics they take in high school will have an influence on the career and higher education options available to them.

The typical pre-college, four-year high school mathematics sequence consists of elementary algebra, geometry, advanced algebra, and pre-calculus (including trigonometry). In the past, the first two years of this sequence were considered sufficient for most students who planned to attend college and major in non-technical fields. Today, however, due to the increased use of quantitative procedures in all fields, a background including advanced algebra is needed for a majority of majors. And completion of the full four-year sequence is essential for majors in science, engineering or mathematics. Furthermore, a strong mathematics background is necessary for an increasing number of fields that require vocational training. To prepare students for the future, schools must focus not only on the basics—they must move their sights beyond the basics.

How Much Mathematics Should Be
Required for High School Graduation?

In *An Agenda for Action* the National Council of Teachers of Mathematics recommends that at least three years of mathematics be required in grades nine through twelve. At the present time, Project Equality of the College Board is addressing this issue and a similar recommendation can be expected.[3] In order to keep career options open, a student should take at least the first three years of the college-preparatory mathematics sequence. Students whose mathematics backgrounds are not sufficient to begin the pre-college sequence in the ninth grade should take basic mathematical skills courses, then enter the sequence as soon as they are ready and go as far as possible. The needs of some students are met by a slowed down sequence—for example a sequence where students can complete elementary algebra in two years rather than one.

Should There Be a Competency Requirement for
High School Graduation?

In recent years many states and local school districts have implemented minimum competency standards in addition to regular course requirements. There is a danger that such competency programs will focus narrowly on computational skills, ignoring today's need for a broader concept of basic skills and the need for students to extend their horizons beyond the basics. On the other hand, schools that do not have a competency requirement sometimes ignore the needs of students who do not enroll in pre-college mathematics courses. Furthermore, there are some important basic skills topics (such as percentages) that tend to get slighted in pre-college courses.

Usually, competency requirements are imposed by forces outside the schools, but school personnel do influence the implementation of such requirements. Externally mandated requirements can be avoided if school staffs prepare in advance and forthrightly address the basic skills competency issue.

What Are the Equity Issues in Mathematics?

Mathematics educators are concerned by the decreasing participation in mathematics courses and the lower achievement in mathematics by females and minorities. Data from national assessment[4] and other sources indicate that achievement of boys and girls is comparable through junior high school, but toward the end of senior high school boys outperform girls on national assessment and Scholastic Aptitude tests. Most of the differences are attributed to avoidance of upper-level high school courses by girls. Enrollment in mathematics is roughly the same for boys and girls until the last two years in high school.[5] In recent years, participation by females in mathematics appears to be increasing.

Black students are seriously underrepresented at all levels of pre-college high school mathematics. Achievement of black and Hispanic students was below achievement of white students on the national assessment mathematics test in 1973 and 1978. The gaps were wider for older students, narrowed for nine-year-old students over the five-year interval, but stayed approximately the same for seventeen-year-olds. Perhaps the introduction of compensatory programs in the elementary schools and the general absence of such programs in secondary schools can help explain these patterns.

Can the Achievement Decline Be Reversed?

On the Scholastic Aptitude Test (SAT), achievement in mathematics decreased from 492 in 1967 to 467 in 1979, a loss of 25 points over the 12 year period. During the same period, verbal scores declined by 39 points. From 1973 to 1978 achievement of seventeen-year-olds declined four points on national assessment mathematics tests. There was essentially no decline in computation, but there were declines of eight or nine points in problem-solving. A challenge for the 1980s will be to see if these downward trends can be reversed, particularly in the area of problem-solving, which the National Council of Teachers of Mathematics recommends as the focus of school mathematics in the 1980s.

How Will Electronic Computing Technology Influence Mathematics Instruction?

While computer literacy should be addressed in a number of subject areas, mathematics teachers will have a major responsibility to provide computer literacy instruction. Today, each school system should develop a comprehensive K-12 program for giving students computer experiences that will prepare them for the world in which they will live. Not all students need to become experts at computer programming, but all students should be able to use computers and understand how computers affect their lives.

The fact that in the "real world" most calculation will be done by computers and calculators implies a change of emphasis in mathematics instruction. The real mathematics of knowing what operations to perform will become more important while the drudge work of complicated computations will be done electronically. Of course, knowledge of basic facts and mental calculation will still be important for setting up problems and checking to see that results are reasonable.

There is fear that the use of calculators will hurt students' ability to compute, but the results of about 100 research studies conducted since 1975 indicate overwhelmingly that the use of calculators helps rather than hinders achievement.[6]

In *An Agenda for Action* the National Council of Teachers of Mathematics recommends that mathematics programs in the 1980s should take full advantage of the power of calculators and computers at all grade levels. To accomplish this, schools will need to provide the hardware, the software, the training of teachers, and the resource and logistical support. Computer use should be imaginative and varied, going beyond the traditional modes of drill and practice or instruction in computer programming. Computers should be used for classroom demonstration of mathematical concepts, for generating tests, worksheets and activities, for constructing mathematical models, for tutorials, for mathematics games and activities, for simulation of applications of mathematics, for solving problems, for scoring tests for processing achievement data, and for a host of other functions. Special courses in computer programming and computer science will be necessary, but the use of computers and calculators should be totally integrated into mathematics instruction at all levels.

Will There Be Qualified Mathematics Teachers?

Because of the increasing demand for people with mathematical backgrounds, there is a growing shortage of certified mathematics teachers in the country. If present and potential mathematics teachers continue to leave teaching for more lucrative opportunities, then the shortage may become severe.

In addition to the need to maintain and improve preservice teacher education, there is a continuing need for inservice education. Certified secondary teachers tend to have sufficient subject matter knowledge, but many lack the teaching skills necessary to address the needs of low achieving, poorly motivated students who exhibit behavior problems and have reading difficulties and other learning problems. Primary teachers, on the other hand, may lack knowledge of how young children learn· mathematics through experience with concrete manipulative materials. Some intermediate and middle school teachers also have weaknesses and anxieties in mathematics that should be addressed. Finally, all teachers will need considerable inservice training to integrate computers and calculators into their mathematics instruction.

How Will Necessary Curriculum Development Be Accomplished?

To meet the changes in mathematics instruction for the 1980s and beyond we will need new objectives, tests and other evaluation techniques for assessing achievement. We will also need curriculum print materials, concrete activities and computer software. The emphasis will probably be more on modifying and improving what we have now than on developing totally new programs as we did in the 1960s.

In the early 1980s federal support for research and development is declining, and states and local school districts are feeling financial pressures. Consequently, new curriculum development will probably be accomplished primarily by commercial publishers. School personnel can influence this development by communicating to publishers what is needed and then being selective about buying; publishers tend to respond to the market.

Will Mathematics Instruction Be a Priority?

In the wake of the Russian Sputnik launching of 1957, mathematics and science received national attention and funding in this country largely through the National tional Science Foundation. In the late seventies mathematics drew further attention at the state and national levels because of public concern about student competencies in basic skills. Today, with the impact of new technology, the public is aware of the increased importance of mathematics. For example, in the 1979 Gallup Poll on Education, mathematics was rated at the top of the list of essential subjects. In spite of declining financial resources for education, there is an increasing demand by the public to focus those resources on basic skills instruction.

II. LEARNING FROM EXPERIENCE AND RESEARCH

Mathematics Achievement Has Increased in Minneapolis

In Minneapolis, as elsewhere in the country, there is concern about achievement. In recent years the only standardized testing in mathematics has been the SRA mathematics test administered near the end of third and sixth grades. In the middle seventies our students scored at grade level at the end of the third grade, but they were below grade level by the end of sixth grade. Now achievement has improved at both levels—from three years, nine months to four years, four months at grade three; and from six years, four months to seven years, three months in computation at grade six. In addition, during 1981 we started administering the California Achievement Test at the end of grade eight. Our median students scored at a grade level of nine years, eight months in both mathematics concepts and computation—a full year above national norms.

What Approach Did We Use to Increase Achievement?

In Minneapolis, the concerns of school administrators helped focus attention on mathematics instruction. Throughout the city, more Title I resources were allocated to mathematics, and in each building there was a greater focus of effort, time and resources on mathematics. Minneapolis has had a strong commitment to alternative schools, so we allowed different schools to develop individual programs. Our general strategy was to get a number of promising practices started, to identify which practices produced the greatest results, and then to replicate those practices in other classrooms. We found the increases in achievement very uneven, with some schools showing dramatic increases (three grade levels or more) and others showing virtually no change. We found many of our greatest increases taking place in Title I schools that traditionally scored well below grade level. Some of these schools were now scoring a year or more above grade level. We looked at these high achieving schools to identify the factors that have contributed to the high achievement.

What Factors Contribute to Achievement?

On the basis of our observations of practices in the high achieving schools, we identified ten factors:
1. Commitment to mathematics instruction
2. High expectation
3. Time on task
4. Leadership
5. Clear objectives with testing to match
6. Systematic approach
7. Skills maintenance
8. Learning materials and teaching strategies
9. Knowledgeable teachers
10. Positive reinforcement

Following the development of this list several years ago, we have seen results of a number of studies on school effectiveness. The results of these studies tend to be in general agreement with our conclusions, thereby increasing our confidence both in the studies and in our observations.

We found leadership to be a particularly important factor. Elementary principals in Minneapolis, as elsewhere, generally lack strong mathematics backgrounds. In schools that showed increased achievement, principals tended to identify a key faculty member to provide leadership and expertise. That person spent at least part time as a mathematics resource teacher for the building, coordinating the program and providing support and training for teachers. The principal's role in identifying and supporting this person was vital.

To help teachers teach to objectives and implement a systematic approach to mathematics instruction, we developed an instructional management system with criterion-referenced tests keyed to objectives. We also provided individual and class profile charts and a prescription index that keyed learning materials to objectives. Implementation was voluntary and about a third of our schools used the system. Some of the schools using our approach quickly showed gains in achievement while others initially did not. Through this experience we came to conclude that an instructional management system is similar to an accounting system. By itself a good accounting system provides information upon which sound decisions can be made, thereby making a profit more likely.

Skills maintenance—the systematic review of previously learned skills—is a factor that nearly always results in increased achievement. We actually learned about the effectiveness of skills maintenance from one of our teachers. Her students showed remarkable gains after she implemented daily reviews. She produced exercises by using COMPUTE, a program developed in Minneapolis that uses a computer to generate exercises. We found that while the computer is helpful, it is not absolutely necessary for skills maintenance. The essential element is frequent maintenance sessions, preferably five to fifteen minutes every day or every other day. Skills maintenance should also include some test-taking skills.

The most important thing that we have learned in Minneapolis is that virtually all students can achieve in mathematics, regardless of socio-economic status, race, family situation, or any other factor. The notion that certain groups of students should be written off is malicious nonsense. We tend to get the kind of achievement we expect.

III. RECOMMENDATIONS

The following recommendations for improving basic mathematical skills instruction are based on research and our experience in Minneapolis.

Establish Competence in Mathematics as a Priority

Every school and school district should have a written policy statement that clearly identifies instruction in basic skills as a priority. This statement—which should specifically identify mathematics (not just computation) as a basic skill—will have impact if it is clearly communicated to administrators, teachers, students, parents, and community and is backed by the allocation of resources.

Assess the Present Situation

Existing data on achievement and enrollment in mathematics should be assessed to determine the strengths and weaknesses of the program. Additional testing and surveys may be required to address unanswered questions. The assessment data should serve to define the problem(s) to be solved.

Develop and Support Leadership

Line administrators, especially building principals, are in key positions to influence instruction. Usually additional curriculum leadership is needed both at the building and district levels. Since mathematics is rarely a curriculum strength of line administrators, they can usually be most effective by identifying and supporting staff leaders with expertise in mathematics. Department chairpersons serve as leaders at the secondary level. A similar type of leadership can be effective at the elementary level. School districts of sufficient size should have mathematics supervisors and resource teachers. These leaders in mathematics should be encouraged to participate in the National Council of Teachers of Mathematics and National Council of Supervisors of Mathematics.

Establish a Climate for Learning

For learning to take place, a school must have an orderly atmosphere and be free of disruptions. The discipline policy should be firm and fair with the aim of leading students from externally imposed discipline to self-discipline. The school should develop an atmosphere that promotes learning and inquiry.

Exhibit High Expectations

Research confirms that expectations become self-fulfilling prophesies. Administrators should therefore convey expectations for high achievement to teachers, students and parents. Teachers in turn should transmit those expectations to students and parents. When everyone believes that achievement can improve and works at it, then it almost invariably does improve.

Identify Clear Objectives with Testing to Match

Research on school effectiveness indicates that achievement is higher in schools where instruction focuses on specific objectives that are known to students, teachers, parents, and administration. Objectives in basic mathematical skills should address all ten skill areas identified by the National Council of Supervisors of Mathematics. In order to diagnose individual student needs, monitor progress and provide for improvement of instruction, testing and other evaluation must match the objectives of the program.

Provide Systematic Instruction That Addresses the Objectives

Instruction should be designed specifically to meet the objectives. Students should be assessed just prior to instruction to determine if they have the necessary prerequisite skills or if they have already mastered some of the objectives. Instruction should then concentrate on closing the gap between what students know and what they are expected to learn. This approach should not preclude open-ended learning that goes beyond the objectives.

Make Provisions for Maintenance of Previously Learned Skills

Probably the most effective way to improve achievement is to implement a skills maintenance program in which previously learned skills are regularly and systematically reviewed. (A five to fifteen minute review every day or every other day is most effective.) It is easier to stop students from forgetting than to let them forget and then teach them over again. Skills maintenance is an excellent transition activity after recess or lunch or at the beginning of a period, and any teacher, from the most progressive to the most conservative, can implement a skills maintenance program with relatively little inservice.

Identify or Develop Appropriate
Learning Materials and Teaching Strategies

Learning materials and teaching strategies should be varied and interesting for students and should focus specifically on the objectives. The selection of materials and strategies should be influenced by research as well as experience. For example, mathematics concepts can be learned through manipulative experiences with concrete materials. The self-paced model for individualizing instruction has tended to be costly and ineffective.[7] On the other hand, practices such as group instruction and cooperative learning show promise for cost-effective instruction in mathematics.

Provide Appropriate Staff Development

Many teachers need to learn how to teach to objectives. Too often we emphasize covering material when we should be uncovering mathematical concepts. Staff development needs should be identified through test data, staff surveys and recommendations of specialists in mathematics education.

Ensure that Students Spend Sufficient Time on Task

Research evidence confirms the common sense observation that the amount of time spent on task strongly influences achievement. At the primary level about forty minutes a day should be allocated for mathematics, while at the intermediate and secondary levels approximately an hour of class time should be used. Time on task is the amount of time students spend actually learning mathematics, both in class and in doing homework. Teaching effectiveness can be increased by carefully structuring class time so that practically all of it is devoted to learning.

Incorporate Technology into the Mathematics Program

Mathematics programs at all levels should take full advantage of the power of calculators and computers. Used effectively in a variety of imaginative ways, these devices will help rather than hinder learning, and students need experience with them in order to develop computer literacy in the computer age.

Provide Students with Information about Mathematics and Their Futures

A key factor in whether a student elects higher level mathematics courses in high school is how useful the course will be. Lack of knowledge about the importance of mathematics in keeping career and education options open can lead to mathematics avoidance. Particular efforts should be made to convey this information to girls and minorities to overcome the stereotype that mathematics is only for the pale and male.

Provide Students and Staff with Positive Reinforcement

Teachers should receive both written and oral praise from their administrators for increases in achievement by their students. Likewise, students should receive praise for achievement from their teachers. Ultimately the most important motivator is one's own knowledge that one has done well. With this in mind, students should receive immediate feedback as to the correctness of their work. Then they can either set out to rectify the mistakes or take pride in the accomplishment and go on to something new.

Use the Results of Evaluation to Improve Instruction

Schools can analyze test results to identify strengths and weaknesses in instruction and to determine the needs of individual students or groups of students. Strong programs, teachers and teaching strategies can be identified through evaluation data; efforts can then be to replicate those strengths in other settings.

Effectively Communicate Priorities, Expectations and Programs

School leaders can set a tone by effectively communicating high expectations for achievement and by stressing the priority of basic skills instruction. Information should be communicated to faculty, students, parents, and the community. When new ideas are being tried it is probably best to give them a low profile until they have proven successful. If they are unsuccessful, then it is easier in the absence of publicity to modify or discard them. Successes should be given a full measure of publicity with credit going to all who contributed.

V. CONCLUSION

The public sees achievement in mathematics as an educational priority, and achievement can be improved significantly by following the recommendations given here. Students from all backgrounds can perform at or above national averages. What we need is school leadership that wants to improve achievement, believes that achievement can be improved and follows through to see that it does improve.

NOTES

1. A copy of the *National Council of Supervisors of Mathematics Position Paper on Basic Mathematical Skills* can be obtained by sending a self-addressed, stamped envelope to Ross Taylor, NCSM Basic Skills, Minneapolis, Minnesota 55413.
2. A copy of *An Agenda for Action: Recommendations for School Mathematics of the 1980s* can be

obtained for $1.00 from the National Council of Teachers of Mathematics, 1906 Association Drive, Reston, Virginia 22091.

3. Project Equality recommendations can be obtained by writing Project Equality, The College Board, 888 Seventh Avenue, New York, New York 10106.

4. Reports on national achievement data can be obtained from National Assessment of Educational Progress, 1860 Lincoln Street, Suite 300, Denver, Colorado 80295.

5. Summaries of national data in science and mathematics are contained in *Science Education Databook*, publication SE80-3, available from The Science Education Directorate, National Science Foundation, Washington, D.C. 20550.

6. Calculator studies information is available from the Calculator Information Center, Room 201, 1200 Chambers Road, Columbus, Ohio 43212.

7. See "Implications of Research for Instruction in Self-paced Mathematics Classrooms" by Harold L. Schoen, in *Organizing for Mathematics*, the 1977 Yearbook of the National Council of Teachers of Mathematics.

PART IV:
READING

READING: THE ART OF THE STATE

Lloyd W. Kline
International Reading Association

What do we know about reading as one of the basic skills being taught in the United States? And, knowing that, where do we go from here?

I wish that questions asked so simply could be answered the same way. In trying to summarize what we know about reading, how does one absorb, integrate, and synthesize the contents of the more than 200 professional journals annotated annually in the *Summary of Investigations Relating to Reading* published by the International Reading Association, which is itself only one of several organizations dedicated solely to the field? Short of being an editor oneself, how does one even begin to gain access to the 1500 manuscripts sent full of hope and consecrated professional truth each year to the journals of that single Association, or to the additional thousands of manuscripts sent to the fifty or more other journals that carry the word *reading* or its concept in their titles? We have not yet asked how to collect and read the thousands of papers presented on the topic of reading at various professional conferences each year, nor how to probe the plans, records, and projects of the hundreds of textbook publishers in the field, nor how to peruse the day-to-day lesson plans of most of the more than two or three million teachers in our schools who give over at least part of their instruction to reading, whether or not they recognize that they are doing so. I have titled my remarks "The Art of the State" with such challenges in mind and with irony aforethought—the state being catatonic, the art magic, and the attempt sheer madness. Whatever I say on the topic, I hereby preface with the disclaimer implied in that truest of sophomore graffiti, ALL GENERALIZATIONS ARE FALSE!

What I shall do in this mad attempt is offer three statements of principle about the teaching of reading that I believe are widely accepted as true, and follow them with three statements of need that I believe we should pursue into the immediate future in the teaching of reading.

Importance of Context

The first statement is one we can support with plenty of empirical evidence, no matter what the specific sub-topic of study within reading: CONTEXT IS ALMOST ALWAYS PREFERABLE TO ISOLATION. That statement is true whether we are talking about interpreting a reading test score out of the context of an individual's total life; or teaching a lesson on the sound of *ph* or the spellings of the schwa out of the context of words and sentences as the learner uses them; or thinking we are experts in language when we consider it out of the context of its many, many levels and uses; or believing we are teaching a youngster to read out of the context of that youngster's expectations, cares, doubts, questions, loves, hates; or extrapolating the results of one small research study out of the context of the mystery and awesomeness by which any of us at random learns to read. Delve into all the research on reading that you can and listen well to all the personal accounts both of learning to read and of teaching it; then, as a teacher, ask yourself next Monday morning, "What are the contexts of what I am about to say or do, and what are the contexts in which and out of which those around me will hear it said or see it done?" Having asked, you will almost certainly teach with greater care, with greater humility, and, one hopes, with greater effectiveness. Teaching letters and sounds out of the context of utterance, utterance out of the context of literature in its broadest sense, literature out of the context of society, of time and place, of life itself, makes your efforts as a teacher but the empty tinkle of brass or sound of cymbal, as the word goes. For this first generalization, empirical evidence abounds from a myriad of sources and sub-topical areas of study: CONTEXT IS ALMOST ALWAYS PREFERABLE TO ISOLATION.

Through the general interest of researchers during much of the recent decade in schema theory, in discourse analysis, in "strings" of letters, in words, and in sentences, one senses a growing consensus that while components of language and the processes of reading and of learning to read can be studied and described in discrete and minuscule detail, the sum of those tiny parts does not necessarily result in effective reading nor in nurturing avid readers. Such reading and such readers always occur in multivariable contexts, social, motivational, cognitive, instructional, what have you, and in sequences that can vary radically from reader to reader, whether we label the reader remedial, developmental, critical, functional, recreational, or gifted. Describing details of the grammatical structures and vocabularies of language and the theoretical sequences of sub-skills of reading offers scholars a scientific shorthand by which they can talk with each other more efficiently about language and about reading, but describing those minute details out of context to a learner struggling to read probably adds to the struggle while detracting from the reading.

Importance of Structure

There is also sufficient empirical evidence for my second statement of what we know about the teaching of reading: STRUCTURE IS USUALLY PREFERABLE TO FRAGMENTATION. We can see this principle at work in studies of discipline in the classroom; in comparison of achievement scores from "more orderly" schools with those from "less orderly" schools, in assessment of attitudes and morale of both students and teachers in various school settings; in the similar levels of effectiveness apparent in vastly different reading programs; in the readiness for learning that students whose lives are in turmoil *fail* to bring to the classroom; in the expressed satisfaction of parents when they are assured their youngsters are safe in school; and in the generally accepted notion that while no specific system of reading instruction works with all students, just about any system works with most. Next Monday morning, bring a sense of order to your classroom by knowing exactly what it is you are trying to do, by letting your students in on that knowledge, and by expecting appropriate behavior of them. Bringing order to the educational process, by the way, does not rule out the creative and divergent, for even if one marches to a different drummer, it is still to the rhythm of a drum, not to the random patter of accident or happenstance.

Perhaps this second principle, that order is preferable to chaos, is simply fret their own children through the anxious years of day-to-day classroom reality. And, for at least fifteen years, the so-called regional laboratories have been at work that universe at any given moment is more than a lucky creature comfort; it is the definition of sanity itself and a key to individual human survival. Little wonder that the principle proves useful and effective in the teaching of reading. It is to gain a sense of order that the teacher of reading needs to understand the structure of language, its component parts, and how they fit together in each of the several theories of language and reading process now current. Even though that teacher need rarely if ever teach those components and theories as such to a class, the structures and theories will underlie the teaching, will give context and purpose and shape to the questioning strategies, to the instructional techniques, to the selection of materials, to the analysis of individual reading problems in that teacher's classroom. A sixth grader need not understand binary mathematics in order to play Asteroids at the local electronic emporium, nor solid-state physics to use the pocket calculator. Neither does that sixth grader need to verbalize intricate principles of phoneme-grapheme relationships in order to read well. At the same time, to clarify what I said earlier about the importance of contexts, it apparently does not work well pedagogically simply to immerse a learner into all contexts at once and hope for the best, sink-or-swim. A sense of order and an active recognition of specific contexts go hand-in-hand in what we know is important and true in reading instruction. To provide that sense of order qualified by context is one of a teacher's primary responsibilities.

Impact of Pluralism

The third principle I suggest we hold about reading has of late taken on renewed, insistent political urgency. Little wonder, since it involves the substances and purposes of reading more publicly and dramatically than do the processes and pedagogy of reading. There is a strong measure of belief among us that PLURALISM IS PREFERABLE TO UNIFORMITY. Arguments about Black English, controversies over teaching English as a second language, disputes over the funding of bilingual programs, battles over book selection and standardized testing have broken well beyond the classrooms and school libraries of America; they are being fought and adjudicated in courtrooms coast-to-coast at an increasing pace and with alarming frequency. Perhaps such litigation represents a turn quite literally to courts of last resort because educators have been so inconclusive and shown so little cohesion among themselves. Our hearts probably unite in the principle so easily stated as pluralism; our heads split open, our brains spill helter-skelter when we attempt to determine precisely what it means to put the principle into practice.

No matter, the principle of pluralism remains a belief common to almost all of us in reading instruction. In *process*, we seek pluralism of theoretical base and solid research in devising our instructional strategies, our program designs, our textbooks, our classroom techniques, our assessments of students' abilities, interests, and achievements. In *substance*, we worry about accommodating those who charge our materials with sexism, racism, ageism, while we try to preserve original texts that have come down to us through the ages. How do we simultaneously serve all the passions, all the persuasions, all the beliefs that humankind falls heir to (heiress to?) when our immediate task as reading teachers is so often simply getting Johnny (Janie?) to read anything at all that appears on our assigned reading list? How do we allot fair measure to each and every individual's sensitivities in ethics and morality without resorting to language and literature so bland, so devoid of morality and ethic and belief and value and substance as to be not worth reading? In *audience*, we agonize over how most effectively and economically to approach the bilingual learner as well as the monolingual, the religious fundamentalist as well as the secular humanist, the child as unique individual in its own natural right as well as that same child as duly ordained legal and moral responsibility of its parents.

Unfortunately and ironically, our attempts to reconcile and serve pluralism have led us too often to pretend there is no morality nor stance in our teaching of reading. We have too often tried to avoid issues of substance rather than confronting within them values in general, or, one might even hope, values held in common among our students. Our failure to understand our shortcoming in that regard, or perhaps simply our frustration at coming to grips with the tough issues and struggles needed to resolve it, or both, have fueled the complaints of many of our most vocal critics. Stephen Arons summarizes the situation in an article in *Saturday Review* (June 1981, page 19): "The loss of consensus complicates the central problem these

45

parents see in professional librarians, professional educators, and the culture in general: the inability to make moral judgments." We cannot dodge these most basic of questions in this most basic of skills, reading: Skills to what ends? What kinds of skills? Levels of skill for what levels of living? Living for what ends? In the very earliest models of American reading instruction, the purposes of reading and the purposes of life were one and the same and easily stated and understood: to love God and to serve Him forever. Even if we were miraculously to get everyone to agree today that God is a he, or indeed that a god exists, the industrial model on which our schools are largely patterned does not ask "What is life?" so often as it asks "What pays off? What is most efficient, as reflected in the mass production of students and of reading scores?"

These questions of process, of substance, and of audience get mixed up quite readily in much of the public mind. One begins, for instance, distrusting secular humanism and ends up carping at any instructional approach other than phonics in the first grade reading program. Or, one dedicates oneself to the innate sacredness of the individual human being within a government of, by, and for everyone, and ends up acquiescing in the massive disruption and imminent dismantling of a public school system that such government has traditionally secured. The jury is still very much out, literally in many cases, with the issues raised by this third statement of mine on where we are in the teaching of reading. But, except in the minds of a sparse few, the principle remains intact across the political spectrum: PLURALISM IS PREFERABLE TO UNIFORMITY. In fact, some of our more dispassionate social observers see right and left meeting on the other side of a full circle in this basic principle, for the purpose behind it is to make the world as safe for me and mine as it seems to be for others. In reading education, there are zealots for this or that approach, advocates for this or that special group of learners, but few of these believers are completely blind to the many visions of truth other than their own.

Need for Educational Engineering

Assuming that the three statements of principle I have offered here indeed reflect the educational state of the art in reading as a basic skill, where do we go from here? What lies ahead? What needs are not being addressed adequately?

I think our first priority as professional reading educators should be a thorough recognition and resolution of the NEED FOR EDUCATIONAL ENGINEERING. In teacher education, curriculum design, classroom organization, materials development, research models, and personnel utilization, we need engineering where almost none now exists. Whether we like the sound of it or not, the truth is that we in America have shaped an educational system according to an industrial model of mass production, but we have yet to develop the engineers that industry has developed to work constantly and productively at bridging the gaps between theory, or "pure" research, and application or practice. Textbook publishers have probably come closest to serving the role of engineers in education, but they have by definition in our society, that is, by the rules of commerce, conformed their products to realities of a mass democratic marketplace as much as to academic theory and research. Educational researchers, by and large, have reflected the medieval traditions that are their heritage as university scholars by disdaining the marketplace, with all its corrupting influences and confounding facts of life. Their medieval forebears depended on the patronage of cardinal or king to butter their bread, allowing them as scholars to dwell honored and secure in their realms of intellectual ivory; the contemporary medievalist counts on a government grant or a foundation handout with which to establish his or her status as master and adorn the surrounding handful of graduate elite with pearls of wisdom (larded occasionally with consultant fees for some of the dirtier work).

Obviously, education suffers from a mismatch, a medieval model securely in place at one level in which researchers and theorists ponder profundities and patiently carry out precious inquiries about the alphas and omegas of reading as process and content, and an industrial model clanking along at another level, churning out a potpourri of students portrayed in endless ranks and files of disarmingly simplistic statistical analysis, while disgruntled teachers, distrustful parents, and dissatisfied taxpayers take turns alternately throwing greaseballs and wrenches into the works. The medieval masters disparage or snub the textbook producers, and quite often they also snub the teachers of teachers, some of whom, by the way, try valiantly to play an engineering role, but without the training or the resources needed for that role. Trainers of teachers, in turn, both preservice and inservice, have probably carried on little research of their own since the completion of whichever graduate degree got them out of the frontlines and into their present positions, where they are trapped between two warring strangers. And, classroom teachers, for their part, tend to cut both medieval masters and teacher trainers out of any sustained dialogue with the immediate and somewhat curt question, "But, what do I do Monday morning?"

With that portrayal of reading education in mind, whether or not I have been entirely fair in drawing it, what kinds of questions might we ask of the educational engineer? What problems might the educational engineer solve? For starters, we could ask for a candid and definitive list of what works well in the industrial model, what works well in the medieval model. Standardized tests and basal readers in the former, certainly; personalization and globalism in the latter, for sure. But, what other advantages inhere in each? What disadvantages? What do the two models have to offer each other? How can they be brought closer together in the educational enterprise? How does the research at Bell Laboratories result in better service in communication for Jody Thompson in Elyria, Ohio? What happens at the Dupont Experimental Station in Wilmington, Delaware, that brings cheaper, stronger polymers to manufacturers and consumers around the world?

A good program of educational engineering will help us to see the forest in spite of our penchant for contemplating trees. In reading clinic after reading clinic, for instance, we take for granted a higher percentage of greater success with worse problem readers than we would ever expect of regular classroom reading instruction. How can we explore that phenomenon so as to apply the facts within it to improving classroom instruction generally? At what costs? With what resources, what configurations of time and space and personnel and materials and equipment?

There are those industries that depend on basic research, research that yields insight or knowledge that is then engineered into successful application in services, products, or information, and we can ask of them what it is they ask of themselves, how they operate. I am sure that one of the questions they raise sooner rather than later in their top research projects is how likely it is that the project will eventually pay off in the marketplace—that is, in services, products, or information. If a project is at least somewhat likely to pay off, approximately when and with what percentage of return on the dollar investment in research and development? If answers along the way seem too negative in light of everything that the enterprise is trying to accomplish within its budget, then the project is dropped, no matter how dear to the hearts of its sponsors or how interesting it may be as a pursuit of knowledge for its own sake. Contrast that rational, considered approach to research and the applied programs that grow out of it with the esoteric laissez-faire approach evident in some of the titles of articles that punctuate many of our professional journals, of presentations that dot many of our professional conferences, of studies that clutter too many editions of *Dissertation Abstracts* in education. If individuals indeed learn to read at varying rates and times and in various sequences, which is almost certainly true, what are the potential implications for classroom instruction, if any, of the last twenty research topics you have seen posed, or of the last twenty lesson plans or curriculum guides you have read? If there are no such implications, and if we have continued to assume "the classroom" as a given in reading instruction, question whether or not the research or the lessons should have been carried out, no matter how clean the design, how rigorous the method of research, how talented the teacher.

Faced with thirty individuals in a hectic classroom, consider the legitimacy of the case study as an engineering problem. Sorry that we cannot engineer a case study for every child every week or so, again assuming that "classroom" is a given, how close can we come to the ideal? What kinds of training and classroom organization would it require, what kinds of administrative support, management, scheduling, staff utilization? Those are questions to be grappled by engineers, not by researchers nor by classroom teachers, nor perhaps even by trainers of teachers, although those who are now in teacher training and supervisory positions seem most conveniently placed to take on engineering roles.

I suspect realistically that all of us at every level could benefit from devoting at least a bit of our professional effort to engineering, even as classroom teachers already develop some of their own instructional materials, and as university scholars fret their own children through the anxious years of day-to-day classroom reality. And, for at least fifteen years, the so-called regional laboratories have been at work in "research and development," perhaps the closest American education has come to establishing an engineering component. Beyond all that, however, what we need, if we persist in following an industrial model in running our schools, is the development of a new profession, that of educational engineering. Like its industrial predecessors, that model will be at least three-tiered, with laboratory engineers, consulting engineers, and field engineers playing their respective roles in analyzing and solving problems of reading instruction, bridging that huge gap between researchers and practitioners.

Changes in Literacy

A second major need we face in reading education is a candid acknowledgment and exploration of the CHANGING SHAPE OF LITERACY, including the computer revolution in communications. There are many time-honored assumptions about reading that we never think of questioning, and much that we do not know about reading and have not yet studied. I am sure that most teachers, consultants, and researchers in the field of reading, for instance, are all but completely unaware of the existence and valuable projects of the Association of American Publishers, or of the Book Industry Study Group which conducts and reports market analysis in the broadest sense. Few if any educators keep up with *Publishers Weekly*, the bible of bookselling, nor do they even know there is such a resource as *Folio: The Magazine for Magazine Management*, both of which would keep them up-to-date on American reading habits and the technology of print production. How many of them realize that every conceivable string of information yet programmed into computers—fantastically complex information manipulable by countless matrices in the most recent equipment—has been rephrased from ordinary discourse into the exclusively yes-no framework of binary logic, that some of those machines now automatically hyphenate words, correct spelling and grammar, and merge functions at one simple keyboard that only a few years ago required three separate departments in the modern office—data processing, word processing, and typography?

McLuhan erred in at least one fundamental way when he proclaimed the obsolescence of print communication fifteen years ago; he failed to foresee the use of the computer as a revolutionary tool that extends those traditional means of communication—reading and writing.

Looking from such points of view outside the education establishment, so to speak, we need not peer into the future to find things we ought to consider but have not. How important is it for curriculum and instruction, motivation and materials development, to recognize that each issue of *Highlights for Children* comes off the press in more copies than there are units of all Beverly Cleary's paperback books in print, or that *Tiger Beat* and *Teen Beat* both rank in the top one-and-a-half percent of circulation among the more than 12,000 magazines currently published in the United States? How much attention should teachers and researchers in reading comprehension and perception give to the fact that magazine designers and art directors are paid at least as much as text editors and infinitely more than writers? Are publishers fooling themselves about what is important in capturing a reader, motivating a reader, communicating with a reader, persuading a reader by visual means alone to part with money for the magazine and be happier and perhaps more knowledgeable for having done so? What does a book provide that a magazine does not? How literate are posters, record covers, graffiti? How many "reading sub-skills" are in play as a youngster electronically battles Space Invaders, scanning the screen, quarter's worth after quarter's worth, for hours on end? Does reading the message on a video screen require the same perceptual skills and the same thought processes, the same instincts and habits, as reading print on paper? How different is it to scroll a message electronically by pressing a button rather than to turn to the next page in a book or magazine? Which sub-skills in reading or writing or mathematics are really basic when the machine in front of you or in your shirt pocket or purse can calculate, compare, scan, or manipulate factual information at your command faster than you can? What remains exclusively the province of print communication, or most appropriate to print rather than to other means of communication?

The shape of literacy is changing, and I am not even confident that reading educators have caught up to the status quo from which the change has been launched. Whether or not the fact seems important to you, a phone company representative can tell you that for the average person, a push-button phone is about 27 percent faster to operate than a conventional dial phone. Should we not at least ask similar kinds of questions of the processes and means of print communication that we claim as our professional specialty?

Morality of Education

Here is my third statement of need as we try to visualize what is ahead educationally in reading as a basic skill: We need a thorough acknowledgment and exploration of the fact that NO SKILL IS AMORAL, and that every fact, every process, every utterance, almost every word, is laden with values to some degree. Yet, in a society that professes Constitutionally to be non-sectarian, what morality, what ethic, what ritual, what system of belief, what professed truth will prove acceptable to all—or to any? I am not sure we need ask nor answer that question that way, but I expanded it and suggested many implications in the third of my earlier statements about where we are in the teaching of reading. Our challenges for the next few years are rather clearly spelled out or implied in that passage. The fact that I choose not to repeat here the several points already offered there should not suggest that this third statement of need is any less urgent nor less heartfelt than the other two.

49

Summary and Recommendations

Reading as a basic skill is doing well in America, quantitatively and probably qualitatively, even within the educational context of an industrial model. Market statistics on numbers of readers and what they are reading counterbalance myopic reading of test scores. John Bormuth calculated in an article in *Visible Language* (Spring 1978) that in the workplace alone reading activities accounted for 23.5 percent of 1972's gross national product. I doubt that the figure has wavered much since then. That estimate does not take into account reading for pleasure, for information outside the workplace, for formal schooling. We have reason enough to bring the full force of our professional, political, economic, and scientific efforts to improving reading as a basic skill. Yet, returning to the title of my remarks, "The Art of the State," it is still true that reading is at least as much art as it is science. It is also still true that the most broadly literate political state is one that boasts a highly civilized society. Firmly rooted in the first truth, let us work confidently toward ever greater realization of the second.

In summary, then, I see reading educators recognizing the importance of context, structure, and pluralism. If we are to move ahead in the teaching of reading as a basic skill, we need a new thrust in educational engineering, accurate description and assessment of contemporary literacy, especially in light of technological developments in communication, and acknowledgment and exploration of pluralism as a philosophy of instruction and as a fact of educational life.

FOUR ESSENTIAL CHANGES
IN COMPREHENSION INSTRUCTION

P. David Pearson
University of Illinois

Reflecting upon the past 15 years in reading education, I am impressed by some significant changes in the concerns of educators about reading instruction.

When I first entered the field, the issues of debate were as follows:

(a) What is the best way to teach beginning reading?

(b) Should the alphabet be taught as a prerequisite to reading instruction?

(c) How can a school build a sound individualized reading program?

Even at that time only a few of my colleagues believed that our energies and efforts should be focused on the comprehension issue. Some even thought that there was little one could do to teach comprehension (believing, I suppose, that it was a matter properly left in the hands of the gods responsible for the genetic transmittal of intelligence).

But times have changed. For better or worse, at least if one is to regard available instructional materials as a barometer of practice, the issue of early reading seems settled. All but a few dust-gathering commercial programs teach phonics early and intensively, even those programs produced by publishers that only a decade earlier systematically delayed phonics until a sizeable number of words had been learned at sight.

Also, it is hard to find commercial reading programs that do not teach the alphabet early. In some, letter sounds as well as letter names are taught prior to that first encounter with real stories.

I mean neither to celebrate nor to condemn the broad consensus on these issues; rather, I only make the observation that broad consensus frees us to examine other issues that may previously have gone unexamined.

Regarding individualization, two kinds of consensus were reached: (1) that progress in reading should be monitored frequently, minutely (note the myriad of specific skills tests at the end of every unit and level in most commercial programs), and individually; and (2) that individualized instruction meant offering practice materials for children to complete individually. Unlike the consensus on early phonics and the alphabet, however, I detect serious discontent in the field about our current practices of individualization. Nonetheless, the energy released from these points of agreement has been directed toward issues of comprehension.

A second reason for the new interest in comprehension comes directly from concerns of practitioners. All too frequently, when meeting with groups of administrators or reading committees from school districts, I encounter this scenario. The group expresses the dilemma of their reading program's test results:

> You know, when we look at our primary grade results we feel good about our program. Our kids are scoring above national norms, which is more than we have a right to expect. Then we look beyond grade 3 and what we find is a gradual slide in those scores, relative to national norms, all the way into high school.

Then this observation is usually followed by a conclusion something like this:

> We must be doing a good job of teaching the decoding skills that characterize the primary grades and a mediocre job of teaching the comprehension skills that characterize the intermediate grades. What can we do about it?

While I welcome this compelling motivation for turning our concerns toward comprehension, I share the concern and frustration of school personnel in that difficult question, "What can we do about it?"

By the way, the recently released data from National Assessment should reinforce this concern. The assessment (NAEP, 1981) indicates that during the seventies, we made excellent progress for nine-year-olds; however, we did not fare well in helping thirteen-year-olds, particularly in test items requiring inferential and interpretive comprehension.

Perhaps the only positive feature of this dilemma is the strength of conviction it can afford us in meeting these concerns about comprehension head-on.

The third factor promoting such concerns stems from a renaissance in psychology. From 1920 to 1965, psychologists, wedded as they were to their behavioristic models, did not study reading. Reading was generally regarded as simply too complex a process to examine, given the constraints of the Stimulus-Response model. But the past decade has witnessed a redirection of perspective among psychologists. Indeed, the relatively new field of cognitive psychology considers the reading process to be one of its most precious objects of study, encompassing as it does sub-processes like attention, perception, encoding, memory, information storage, and retrieval.

At any rate, psychology has returned to one of its rightful homes: the study of reading. Reading education has benefited greatly from the return, for the new cognition has provided a wealth of ideas and hypotheses that educators can use to create hypotheses worthy of testing in the ultimate laboratory—the classroom.

These three forces (consensus on other matters, heightened concern about comprehension failures, and a new set of intellectual challenges), then, have converged to create an atmosphere in which attention within the reading field has focused on comprehension.

In brief, here are the changes I propose:
1. We must change the kinds of questions we ask about selections children read.
2. We must change our attitude toward and practices of reading vocabulary.
3. We must change the way we teach comprehension skills.
4. We must change our conception of the role of the teacher in the reading program.

Changing Questions

Durkin (1978-79) and her co-workers spent some 17,997 minutes observing reading lessons in intermediate grade classrooms. One of the conclusions she drew from these observations was that teachers spend a sizable portion of time in which they interact with students during reading classes asking questions. Students, conversely, spend lots of time answering questions. Furthermore, these assessment sessions (Durkin's term for this kind of interaction) tended to be characterized by relatively low-level questions in search of single correct answers. We've all seen this; probably most of us, myself included, have done it. I ask a question. I call upon Suzie. She gives an answer other than the one I had in mind. I turn toward Tommy. He gives a second answer, but still not the one I had in mind. My head bobs from student to student until someone finally gives the answer I was looking for. It's a game called "Guess what's in my head!"

When Durkin (1981) turned from classroom observation to teacher's manuals, she discovered a remarkably similar situation—much space devoted to story questions, many low-level questions in search of single correct answers (*and* manuals that provided correct answers to each comprehension question, save those that invited almost every response as a correct answer).

Beck and her colleagues (Beck, McKeown, McCaslin, & Burkes, 1979) have also examined teacher's manual questions. Reading Beck's analysis of questions, one is struck by another facet of the questions in manuals. They appear to have been written using the committee assignment approach. It's as though six people were assigned the task of generating questions for a story. And they decided to accomplish the task using three guidelines: (a) each was assigned one page of a six-page test; (b) they could ask questions that *either* had explicit answers stated in the text *or* had nothing in particular to do with the text; and (c) none of them was allowed to look at any page other than her own or to consult anyone else about the questions she generated. The apparent result of this approach is a random barrage of questions that don't cohere one with another. They don't form a *line* of questions.

Thus far the evidence presented suggests that the questions asked about typical basal reader questions (1) are more random than coherent, (2) focus either on trivial detail or irrelevant asides, and (3) do little to foster an integrated conception of either what the particular story is about or what stories in general are about.

Beck et al. do suggest a way out of this situation. They argue, after examining recent research about story comprehension, that teachers need to develop, prior to question generation, a story map for each story children are asked to read. A story map, according to Beck, consists of a specification of the main character's problem in the story and attempts to solve that problem, leading, eventually, to a resolution. Having generated such a map, teachers would develop questions that elicit some major component of the story map. Questions that elicit either too general or too specific responses are not to be allowed. The flow of the story, from inception to resolution, serves as the paramount criterion for question inclusion.

Translated into practical issues regarding basal reading questions, Beck's analysis suggests that guided reading questions (those page-by-page questions in grades one and two or those immediately following questions in grades three and up) should be limited in such a way that they elicit only major components of a story map.

Indeed, recent research evidence (Beck, Omanson, & McKeown, 1981; Gordon, 1980; Singer & Donlan, 1981) validates exactly such a notion. Questions that focus student attention on important story elements elicit better comprehension and/or story recall as well as better recall of new stories for which no questions are asked. Apparently, the systematic application of such a framework for story comprehension helps students develop what might be called a generic "story understander."

So much for guided reading questions. What about those questions that teachers typically ask in pursuit of building background for story comprehension before students read? Here we have considerable evidence to guide our search for commendable practices. Hansen and Pearson (Hansen & Pearson, 1980; Hansen, 1981; Hansen & Pearson, in press) have conducted several studies examining the effect of story questions, particularly with reference to enhancing children's ability to answer inferential comprehension questions. Two findings in their line of research are relevant to our concerns. First, they find that simply making sure that guided reading questions (those questions asked either during or after stories) include many inference questions enhances both story specific inferential comprehension *and* comprehension of new stories. Second, they find that the additional provision of prereading questions that focus on inferences to prior knowledge coupled with specific instruction in *how* to generate answers to such questions and *why* such comprehension is important leads to even better inferential comprehension of stories. In short, the available data suggest it matters a great deal what kind of questions we use to prepare children for story comprehension: a set for predicting, relating text to prior knowledge, and evaluating predicted outcomes is superior to a more literal/factual orientation.

In trying to reconcile the available data on what promotes better understanding of textbook selections with conventional practices, I have derived the following instructional guidelines for asking questions. Remember that some of these guidelines bear the grace of evidence, some "make sense," and others are best guesses:

1. Ask lots of "have you ever . . . ?" questions in trying to build story background.
2. Then, try to elicit predictions about what story characters will do in similar circumstances.
3. Ask purpose setting questions that, to be answered, require a complete reading of a selection.
4. Immediately after reading, return to the purpose.
5. Guided reading questions should focus on the story map.
6. Reserve comparison questions (with prior knowledge and/or other stories) to a second skimming of the story.
7. Reserve author's craft questions for that same second (or even third) skim.

So much for questions. Now to vocabulary.

Vocabulary Instruction

Dale Johnson and I have been so concerned about vocabulary instruction that we decided to write a book exclusively devoted to the topic. Our main concerns in that book are twofold: (1) that people will recognize the primacy of *meaning* vocabulary over *word recognition* vocabulary, and (2) that they will embrace our philosophy of *ownership of a word's meaning* over *facility at defining the word*. Let me explain with an anecdote:

A few years ago a student teacher brought in a lesson plan and some student papers from a reading lesson he had taught to some fifth grade students, remarking, "Let me tell you about my great vocabulary lesson."

"What did you do?" I asked with anticipation.

"Well first I had them look up the new words in their pocket dictionaries . . ."

"And then? . . ."

"I knew you'd ask that," he added firmly. "And then I asked them to write the words in sentences."

"Can I see some student papers?" I asked. The first word on the first paper was *exasperated*. The student had written, for a definition, *vexed*. And his accompanying sentence was, *He was exasperated.*

At that point, all the student knew was that the child could find the word in the dictionary, could copy the first available definition, and could recognize that a word ending in -*ed* could serve in the past participle slot in a sentence. He knew nothing about whether the child knew the meaning of the word; he knew nothing about whether the child *owned* the word, to use Beck's (1981) term for what it means to acquire a new vocabulary item.

The problem illustrated here is similar to the dilemma faced by teachers each time they find a new list of vocabulary words for a new reading selection (or when they come to a new chapter in a social studies or science textbook). How much concept development needs to be done *before* children will be able to (a) understand the text at hand and/or (b) use that new vocabulary when they read new and different texts?

While we do not have the final answer to these questions, we can derive some guidelines from recent research on the relationship between knowledge about a topic and comprehension of texts related to that topic. First, there is no question about that relationship: a reader's knowledge about a topic and particular key vocabulary to be included in a text to be read is a better predictor of comprehension of that text than is any measure of reading ability or achievement (Johnston & Pearson, in press; Johnston, 1981). Second, several studies point to the advantage of a full-blown concept development approach to vocabulary over a more conventional definition and sentence approach (*if* students needed any help at all with the vocabulary). This finding is especially salient for subsequent inferential comprehension tasks (Schachter, 1978; Adams & Carnine, in press). Particularly useful have been semantic mapping and semantic feature analysis approaches (Thoms, in press)—the kind Johnson and Pearson (1978) discuss, as well as other approaches that emphasize semantic elaboration (Adams & Carnine, in press; Beck, Perfetti, & McKeown, 1982). What these more useful approaches have in common is their emphasis on where a word *fits* in children's semantic repertoire rather than what it means or how it is used in sentences. That is what it means to "own" a word—to know how it is like and how it is different from other words which a child already knows.

In order to accomplish this goal for vocabulary, we must alter our stance toward vocabulary instruction. We must change the questions we ask when we get ready to help a child acquire a new concept. Too often we have asked,

What is it the children don't know and how can I get that into their heads?
The better question is,

What is it that the children *do* know that's enough like the new concept so that I can use it as an anchor point?

We can learn new concepts only in relationship to concepts we already possess. This is a principle that we use all the time with our peers when we explain a new phenomenon. We say,

Well it's sort of like X . . . but . . .
We establish a contact with a known concept; then we explain how it's different from the known concept. Why we do not extend the same courtesy to children I do not understand. Somehow in schools we seem to prefer definition to explanation. Until and unless we refocus our vocabulary efforts on techniques emphasizing semantic elaboration and semantic fit, we shall never achieve the goal of ownership that I think we would all like to achieve.

Comprehension Skill Instruction

When Durkin (1978-79) completed her classroom observation study, one of her goals was to determine when, how, and how often teachers engaged in direct, explicit instruction for comprehension skills; that is, what did teachers tell students about how they should perform the various comprehension tasks assigned on the myriad of worksheets and workbook pages in their reading programs? Of those 17,997 minutes, she found precisely 45 minutes devoted to this kind of direct instruction in comprehension (and 11 minutes of that was on the influence of punctuation). She found much of what she labeled mentioning—saying just enough about an assignment so that students understood the formal requirements of the task, but stopping short of demonstrating *how* to solve the task cognitively, or *what* to look for in the task as clues for generating a solution.

Recently Durkin (1981) conducted a similar analysis of basal manuals, looking for instances of comprehension instruction. While the manuals fared somewhat better than the teachers, they still fell woefully short of what we might want to call substantive instruction. Most of these instructional directives consisted of a single sentence: "Tell the students that the main idea is the most important idea in the paragraph." Rarely was much in the way of modeling, guided practice, or substantive corrective feedback suggested. Again, Durkin felt that "mentioning" better characterized what the manuals were offering in the way of instructional directives to teachers: saying just enough about the skill so that students could complete the workbook or worksheet task, but stopping short of offering any strategy for *how* to complete the task.

Perhaps both teachers and manuals offer little direct instruction in how to solve comprehension tasks because comprehension is such a complex interactive process— i.e., influenced by so many situational and individual factors that it simply does not lend itself to the development of simple generalizations about either *what* these so-called comprehension skills are or *how* any individual should go about applying a general skill to the variety of texts and testing formats he or she might encounter. Furthermore, one might argue that application of a comprehension skill to a particular text is so dependent upon these idiosyncratic factors (the difficulty of that text, any particular student's knowledge of the topic addressed in that text, and that reader's interest and motivation for reading that text) that any hope of discovering general rules or heuristics for how one *finds a main idea, determines a sequence,* or *distinguishes fact from opinion* is doomed. In other words, there may be no context-free generalizations about comprehension comparable to the rules we teach children for decoding unknown words (e.g., the silent *e* rule, the vowel digraph rule, or the open and closed syllable rules). If one accepts such a context-bound orientation (which is comparable to saying that the ability to apply any given skill is determined by the total context in which it is to be applied), then perhaps all one can do is make certain that students receive many opportunities to apply the skill to a variety of texts and workbook pages. Indeed, the findings of Durkin's two studies suggest that just such a rationale could be behind what we find in current educational practice.

An alternative (and instructionally more hopeful) view is that up until the present time we simply haven't understood the comprehension process well enough to be able to identify and define basic and distinct comprehension skills, let alone determine strategies that teachers could offer students for applying these skills consistently across the range of texts and practice activities they are likely to encounter. Viewed from the traditional concept learning perspective we were all exposed to in basic psychology and/or educational psychology courses, we can restate our dilemma by suggesting that we have yet to learn what the "concepts" of each of these skills are; consequently, we are hard-pressed to teach those "concepts" to children.

Consider what we typically mean when we say a person possesses a concept of a *dog* or a *cat* or a *classroom*. For us, the critical test of concept learning is that the person who possesses it can identify new stimuli in the environment that either *are* or *are not* examples of the concept. Concepts, in other words, are *context-free*. A person who possesses a concept of a dog can recognize dogs and non-dogs regardless of whether the stimuli are observed in kennels, dining rooms, or airplanes; or whether the dog is large, small, or about average; or whether its ears are long or short, etc.

By analogy, to say that a student possessed a concept of main idea would require that he or she be able to determine the main idea of a text segment whether the text was about plants, animals, or outer space; whether the main idea was stated early, late or not at all; whether the main idea was in the form of a title, a heading, or a sentence embedded within the text. Further, the student would have to be able to distinguish a main idea from a detail or an irrelevant statement. And we would probably expect that the student possessed, and maybe was able to state explicitly, some criteria for selecting or creating main ideas and distinguishing them from things that were not main ideas. Only then would we be sure that the concept was both operational and context-free.

Whether or not "concepts" for comprehension skills can ever be learned by students or taught by teachers I am not certain. However, some recent developments in instructional research regarding reading comprehension lead me to believe that we can help students, even the hard-to-teach students, approximate such concepts.

I'm not certain that I want to bestow the label "concept" upon what students have learned in these instructional studies; perhaps the label "heuristic strategy" is more apt (a friend of mine defines a heuristic strategy as a rule that doesn't work so well). Now heuristics, according to the Oxford English Dictionary, is the art of discovery or invention. Such a definition is appropriate to the studies I am about to describe because what I think these researchers have been able to give to students are strategies for discovering some regularities across different texts, tasks, and situations.

Hansen (1981)—the study mentioned in the earlier section about questions—set about to determine whether she could improve second grade students' ability to answer questions that did not have explicit answers in the texts (what we usually call inferential comprehension). She began with two hypotheses about why literal comprehension performance is usually superior to inferential comprehension performance: (a) students simply may not get sufficient opportunity to practice drawing inferences, or (b) they simply do not know how to go about generating answers that are not explicitly stated in the text. She developed an experimental treatment to evaluate each hypothesis. A control group received, for guided reading and follow-up discussion questions, the conventional mix of about 80% literal to 20% inferential questions. A question-only experimental group received *all* inferential guided reading and follow-up discussion questions. A strategy-training experimental group received a pre-reading strategy training designed to sensitize students to the importance of using their own experiences to predict and evaluate story characters' problems and actions. Very much in the tradition of the Directed Reading-Thinking Activity (DRTA), the treatment required students (a) to state what they would do in situation X and (b) to predict what a particular story character might do. After recording their *own* responses and predictions about characters on strips of paper, students wove the strips together—a sort of physical metaphor for comprehension as a process of weaving together what one already knows with what is new in a text. Students in this strategy training group received some guided reading questions as did the control group. In terms of the typical instructional sequence for a lesson, the special strategy training replaced the traditional building background and purpose setting segment. In *all* other aspects, the three groups received identical instruction for the 10 stories.

Using a variety of outcome measures to evaluate treatment effects, Hansen found that both treatments (practice-only and strategy training) produced reliable increases in the second grade students' ability to answer inferential comprehension questions, at no loss to their performance on literal tasks. In fact, measures taken after reading each of the stories in which the instruction was embedded indicated that the strategy group actually outperformed the control group on literal comprehension questions. Apparently what happened was that students *either* exposed to many questions requiring answers from prior knowledge *or* given a strong *set* toward using prior knowledge to predict and evaluate story events learned that it was legitimate to invoke one's prior knowledge in generating answers to questions. Several students actually volunteered that prior to the training they did not know that it was "o.k." to use "their own words" to answer questions. In addition, the strategy training appeared to increase depth of processing in such a way that students paid more attention to the literal message of the text as well as to the relationship of that message to their own knowledge structures, at least for those stories in which the teacher implemented the strategy training.

In a second, related study, Hansen and Pearson (in press) combined the two treatments (strategy training and many inferential post-reading questions) and compared the hybrid to a "business as usual" control group for both good (average reading test scores about 6.3) and poor (average about 3.2) fourth grade students. In addition, they trained teachers to administer the treatments instead of having the experimenters do so. Also, they added a new metacognitive dimension to the training. Before each training session, they reminded students of what it was they were doing prior to each story (using prior knowledge to predict story events) and why. Dependent measures involved answering new questions for both the stories in which the instruction was embedded as well as new stories for which instruction was not provided.

After 10 weeks of training, few differences emerged among good readers; however, strong and reliable differences surfaced among the poor readers. In each case these differences favored the hybrid inference training group. In fact, on one measure, the poor experimental students performed as well as the good control students despite a 3-year grade norm difference in average reading test scores. Experimental-control differences were observed on both literal and inferential measures but were more striking on the inferential.

Hansen and Pearson concluded that the training was most effective for precisely that subset of students who typically exhibit frustration in performing comprehension tasks. The lack of consistent reliable differences among good readers might, they thought, be attributed to the fact that good readers often discover such strategies on their own through sheer exposure to various tasks. Poor readers appear to require more careful guidance from a teacher. Informal data confirmed the legitimacy of this observation from the Hansen (1981) study; that is, many children were surprised to learn that it was acceptable to give an answer not explicitly stated in the text. Also, teachers who participated in the study expressed great satisfaction with the experimental treatment, stating that their reading group discussions were more lively and interesting (they also expressed some concern about getting used to the treatment, the variety of responses offered, and the difficulty of generating good inference questions).

Gordon (1980) continued this general line of inference training research by developing and evaluating an even more explicit technique for helping children become better at drawing inferences. In her training procedure, she led groups of fourth grade students through the following training stages over an eight-week period:

STAGE 1: Teacher asks an inference question, gives an answer, shows students where she got the clues in the text that support the answer.

STAGE 2: Teacher asks question, gives answer, has students discover sensible clues.

STAGE 3: Teacher asks question, gives clues; students generate answer.

STAGE 4: Teacher asks question; students develop both answer and text clues.

These steps vary along a continuum of responsibility for task completion. In Stage 1, the teacher takes all the responsibility. In Stage 4, the student takes most of the responsibility. In a sense, Stage 1 represents modeling, and Stage 4, independent practice or application. Stages 2 and 3 represent guided practice. Campione (1981) has suggested that instruction can be conceptualized as what happens in those intermediate stages between total teacher responsibility (modeling) and total student responsibility (practice or application).

On outcome measures (answers to literal and inferential questions) derived from the selections in which the instruction was embedded, students receiving this explicit strategy for how to generate inferences outperformed two other experimental treatments, one involving a set toward general story understanding and another involving a set toward creative language activities. On transfer measures, i.e., stories for which no instruction was provided, this same treatment outperformed the other groups, but only on questions requiring inferences to prior knowledge.

Ironically, Gordon's work also suggested that the group that received the story schema training (attention to the content and *structure* of stories) was able to recall much more of the basic event structure of transfer stories than was the inference training group. What this finding suggests is that the results of training are relatively strategy-specific; that is, children learn what we teach them and ask them to practice. This finding, however, should be viewed as encouraging because it suggests that if we can add specific strategy training to what we presently offer students (much independent practice), we can ameliorate prose comprehension. The only caution we might add is that we should not expect any single training element to solve all our problems. Breadth of coverage may be as important as depth of coverage; however, breadth alone will not do the job, as is evidenced by our present circumstance (much varied practice) in American education with respect to comprehension.

Raphael and Pearson (in press) have focused training upon students' ability to vary their strategies for generating answers to questions as a function of the task demands of the question (Does it look like I should go to the text or to my head for an answer?) in relationship to the information available (What does the text say about this? and What do I already know about the issue?). Using Pearson and Johnson's (1978) trichotomy classifying question-answer relations (text-explicit, text-implicit, and script-implicit), they taught fourth-, sixth-, and eighth-grade students to discriminate situations where both question and answer come from the same sentence in the text (example 2), where the question and the answer come from different parts of the text (example 3), and where the question is motivated by the text but the answer comes from the reader's prior knowledge (example 4).

(1) Matthew was afraid Susan would beat him in the tennis match. He broke both of Susan's rackets the night before the match.
(2) Who was afraid? Matthew.
(3) Why did Matthew break both of Susan's rackets? He was afraid Susan would beat him.
(4) Why was Matthew afraid? Maybe Susan was a better player.

They taught the children to label these three strategies RIGHT THERE, THINK and SEARCH, and ON MY OWN, respectively. During five 45-minute sessions, they asked students to answer questions and then decide which of the three strategies they had used to generate their answers. From lessons 1-5, children received increasingly longer texts, more questions, and increasingly less modeling and feedback from the teachers. In short, the instructional sequence for this short series of lessons followed Campione's (1981) continuum. Outcome measures involved reading new selections and answering questions inviting each of these three response generation strategies.

Compared to an orientation-only group (these students learned the system in a 20-minute orientation but did not receive the systematic instruction, practice, and opportunity to make judgments about the strategies they had used) and, subsequently (Raphael, 1982), a no treatment control, the trained students were superior on both the number of quality answers they provided and on their ability to judge what kinds of strategies they had used. In other words, they were better both at comprehending and monitoring their own comprehension. While patterns of superiority varied across ability groups (that is, different ability groups gained differentially on different question-answering tasks), the training was effective for all ability groups and all grade levels. Apparently, the students gained some control over strategy use and resource allocation. Like students in the Hansen and Pearson (in press) study, one student said, when he learned about the ON MY OWN strategy, "I never knew I could get answers from my head before."

Brown and Palincsar (in press) have applied a somewhat different strategy for helping learning disabled junior high students generate better answers to inference questions. What is particularly interesting in this work is the interaction between teacher and student in the individualized training. The teacher begins by modeling; she gives an answer and then describes what she did to generate the answer (in short, she makes explicit her reasoning strategy). Then she asks the student to do the same. Finally she switches student and teacher roles so that the students are, in a sense, put in charge of comprehension monitoring. Her training paradigm resulted in large improvements for these learning disabled students, and the training proved durable over an extended period of time.

Raphael (1982) has extended her research by training teachers to apply her strategy and materials over an eight-week training period. A preliminary analysis of her findings suggests that students trained by her participating teachers made substantial gains in their ability to answer all kinds of questions.

This group of students suggests the possibility that comprehension can be taught after all. They also suggest that what is missing in our current milieu (what I like to call our practice-only approach to comprehension) is the critical element of the teacher interacting with groups of students to help them gain more personal control over the instructional environment in which we place them.

Changing Role for Teachers

Taken together, these first three changes that I am advocating imply a fourth more general change in our prevailing model of the role of the teacher in the educational environment.

The model of a teacher implicit in the practices of the seventies was that of a manager—a person who arranged materials, tests, and the classroom environment in such a way that learning could occur. But the critical test of whether learning did occur was left up to the child and the materials. Children practiced applying skills: If they learned them, fine; we always had more skills for them to practice; if they did not, fine; we always had more worksheets and ditto sheets for that same skill. And the most important rule in such a mastery role is that practice makes perfect, leading, of course to the ironic condition that children spent most of their time working on precisely that subset of skills they performed least well.

Why did we embrace such a model? There were several forces at work. First, the press for accountability and minimal competencies forced us to be accountable for something. And we opted for all the bits and pieces rather than the entire reading process. Second, the notion of mastery learning, presented so elegantly by Bloom (1968) and Carroll (1963), made such a system seem reasonable to us. Third, our friends in publishing unwittingly aided and abetted the movement by providing seductively attractive materials and management schemes. The fascination with materials has become so prevalent that, in a recent survey, Shannon (1981) found that virtually all of the administrators and a high proportion of teachers believe that materials *are* the reading program.

I'd like to propose a new model for the eighties: a model in which the teacher assumes a more central and active role in providing instruction, a model in which practice is augmented by direct teacher modeling, guided practice and substantive feedback, a model in which the teacher and the child move along that continuum of task responsibility I discussed earlier, a model that says just because we want students to end up taking total responsibility for task completion does not mean that we should begin by giving them total responsibility. (If we do this, by the way, we will be taking the mastery notions of Bloom and Carroll more seriously than ever before because additional teacher assistance was, along with time on task, one of the components in their models. We will also be recognizing that true individualization has never meant that instruction is delivered individually, only that progress is monitored individually and that what may be best for a given individual is not another worksheet but perhaps a live body present to provide the guidance and feedback it will take to bring students to independent levels of performance.) As a metaphor for this new model, I'd like to replace the teacher as manager metaphor with a metaphor of the teacher as teacher. I know the idea is not startlingly fresh, but it does have a nice ring to it.

REFERENCES

Beck, I. Developing Comprehension: The impact of the directed reading lesson. In R. Anderson, J. Osborn, & R. Tierney (Eds.), *Learning to read in American schools: Basal readers and content texts.* Champaign, Ill.: Center for the Study of Reading, 1981.

Beck, I. L., McKeown, M. G., McCaslin, E. S., & Burkes, A. M. *Instructional dimensions that may affect reading comprehension: Examples from two commercial reading programs.* Pittsburgh: University of Pittsburgh, Learning Research and Development Center, 1979.

Beck, I. L., Omanson, R. C., & McKeown, M. G. *A study of instructional dimensions that affect reading comprehension.* Paper presented to the American Educational Research Association, Los Angeles, April 1981.

Beck, I. L., Perfetti, C. A., & McKeown, M. G. *The effects of long-term vocabulary instruction on lexical access and reading comprehension. Paper submitted for publication, 1982.*

Bloom, B. S. *Learning for mastery. Evaluation Comment,* 1968, *1*(2), 1-12.

Brown, A. L., & Palinscar, A. S. Inducing strategic learning from texts by means of informed, self control training. *Topics in Learning & Learning Disabilities,* in press.

Campione, J. *Learning, academic achievement and instruction.* Paper presented at the Center for the Study of Reading pre-IRA Conference, New Orleans, April 1981.

Carrol, J. A model of school learning. *Teacher's College Record,* 1963, *64,* 723-733.

Durkin, D. What classroom observations reveal about reading comprehension instruction. *Reading Research Quarterly,* 1978-79, *14,* 481-533.

Durkin, D. Reading comprehension instruction in five basal reading series. *Reading Research Quarterly,* 1981, *16,* 515-544.

Gordon, C. J. *The effects of instruction in metacomprehension and inferencing on children's comprehension abilities.* Unpublished doctoral dissertation, University of Minnesota, 1980.

Hansen, J. *The effects of inference training and practice on young children's comprehension. RRQ,* 1981 *16,* 391-417.

Hansen, J., & Pearson, P. D. *The effects of inference training and practice on young children's comprehension* (Tech. Rep. No. 166). Urbana: University of Illinois, Center for the Study of Reading, April 1980. (ERIC Document Reproduction Service No. ED 186 839)

Hansen, J., & Pearson, P. D. *An instructional study: Improving the inferential comprehension of fourth grade good and poor readers* (Tech. Rep. in press). Urbana: University of Illinois, Center for the Study of Reading.

Johnston, P. *Background knowledge, reading comprehension and test bias.* Unpublished Ph.D. disertation, University of Illinois, 1981.

Johnston, P., & Pearson, P. D. *Prior knowledge, connectivity, and the assessment of reading comprehension* (Tech. Rep.). Urbana-Champaign: University of Illinois, Center for the Study of Reading.

National Assessment of Educational Progress. *The National Assessments of Reading: Changes in Performance, 1979-80* (Report No. 11-R-01). Education Commission of the States, Denver 1981.

Pearson, P. D., & Johnson, D. D. *Teaching reading comprehension.* New York: Holt, Rinehart, & Winston, 1978.

Raphael, T. E. *Training teachers to train students to monitor their question answering strategies.* Manuscript in preparation, 1982.

Raphael, T. E., & Pearson, P. D. *The effects of metacognitive strategy awareness training on students' question answering behavior* (Tech. Rep.). Urbana-Champaign: University of Illinois, Center for the Study of Reading, in press.

Shannon, P. *Teachers self-perceptions and reification of instruction within reading instruction.* Unpublished doctoral dissertation, University of Minnesota, 1981.

Singer, H., & Donlan, D. Active comprehension: Problems solving schema with question generation for comprehension of complex short stories. *Reading Research Quarterly,* in press.

THE TEACHING OF READING TO LANGUAGE-MINORITY STUDENTS: SOME BASIC GUIDELINES

Rosalinda Barrera
New Mexico State University

As the number of language-minority[1] children steadily increases in American schools in all localities—urban, rural, suburban—the issue of how to teach reading more effectively to these students remains a pressing concern for many educators. We do well to ask what knowledge has been gathered in the past decade by reading-language studies and large scale bilingual education programs that can help us provide better reading instruction for this growing population of learners.

From a search of literature and from my own experiences in reading education, I have formulated three generalizations that subsume the many recent insights about the teaching of reading to language-minority learners. I present these generalizations here as basic guidelines for strengthening current and future reading programs for these students. Briefly stated, if reading instruction is to be most effective and relevant for language-minority students, it must (1) take into account a complex of factors, within as well as beyond the classroom; (2) be grounded in a comprehensive and coherent view of language and literacy; and (3) transcend a "remedial" perspective.

Unfortunately, as fundamental as these three points are, I don't see them reflected in much of the reading instruction that now reaches language-minority learners. Therefore, we should not only examine the nature of these points, but should think about how we can begin to translate them into reading program realities. Those are the objectives I have set out for this paper.

ACKNOWLEDGING COMPLEXITIES AND REALITIES

In any discussion of the reading education of language-minority children, language is bound to be a central consideration. However, this does not mean that the entire matter of teaching reading to language-minority children can or should be viewed solely in terms of language. We know that factors other than language—such as social, political, attitudinal, and programatic factors—also play a role in learning, and, therefore, should be considered in planning reading instruction for language-minority children.

Initial Reading Instruction

Certainly, the beginning reading instruction of language-minority children is crucial in their reading education, greatly affecting all subsequent learning. Here a basic question is whether the limited- or non-English-speaking child should be taught to read through his native language first and then English, or in English only, or through both languages simultaneously. Although from a reading/learning perspective, it makes good "reading sense" to teach the child to read in that language which is most familiar to him (Goodman, 1976), one cannot overlook factors that might preclude using the native language for initial reading instruction. Some of these factors include the lack of a home literacy tradition in the native language, or even overt parental disapproval of native-language literacy; inadequate personnel or materials to support a quality program of native-language literacy; and unsupportive community and school attitudes toward native-language literacy (Goodman, Goodman & Flores, 1979). In the presence of these factors, the question of whether to use the native language for beginning reading has to be weighed very carefully.

Clearly, the factor of language or, more specifically, language of instruction cannot stand alone as the only consideration in planning a reading program for the language-minority student.

By the same token, if we favor an English-only route to initial reading for the language-minority child, we cannot assume that the use of English for instruction will by itself translate into quality reading instruction. (Here again notice the paring down of a complex educational question to consideration of language only.) Many other factors must be considered. For example, contemporary reading research repeatedly shows the importance of the learner's experience and background knowledge, including his or her cultural schemata, in reading comprehension (Steffensen, Joag-dev, & Anderson, 1979; Santa, 1981; Goodman & Goodman, 1978). Likewise, research has linked reading achievement by language-minority youngsters to school social factors, such as the nature of teacher-pupil interaction (Au & Mason, 1981; Cazden, 1981). It is simplistic to think that the English reading education of language-minority children, whether these children are beginning readers or already literate in their native language, will be improved significantly if factors such as these are overlooked.

A Kaleidoscope of Factors

When one recognizes the many factors surrounding the reading education of language-minority children, it is apparent that there can be no across-the-board responses or simple solutions in this matter. What may be desirable for the reading instruction of one group in one area (e.g., Spanish-speaking children in Florida) may not be as desirable for another group in another area (e.g., Pueblo children in New Mexico). In this case, one situation might support a native-literacy instruction model; the other might lend itself only to an English as a second language (ESL) instruction model. In line with this, one should not be too quick to generalize about the second-language learning of one group of students (e.g., English-speaking Canadian children learning French) based on another group of students (e.g., Navajo children in Arizona learning English) without taking into account socioeconomic, political, legal, and other factors. All in all, we must be sensitive to a kaleidoscope of factors—educational and non-educational, complex and interrelated—as we plan, implement, and try to improve reading instruction for language-minority students. More than likely, to think in lesser terms is to jeopardize the quality of instruction.

DISPELLING SIMPLISTIC NOTIONS

It is often the case that in whatever setting language-minority children receive reading instruction—be it bilingual or monolingual English classroom—certain simplistic notions about their language and literacy learning prevail. Needless to say, these notions are largely incompatible with modern insights and findings about language, reading, and the learner. It hardly needs saying, too, that these instructional beliefs and the classroom practices they engender are often more counterproductive than supportive of the literacy development of these students. To build quality reading programs for language-minority students we must subject these questionable notions and practices to careful scrutiny and rethinking (Barrera, in press).

The Reading Process

Especially when working with children for whom the school language is a second language, we cannot afford to embrace narrow or simple views of the reading process. We cannot reduce the reading act to merely calling out words or relating sounds to letters. If such a view underlies second-language reading instruction, then teachers are likely to grossly misunderstand children's reading abilities, focusing wrongly on pronunciation or other surface aspects of reading at the expense of comprehension and meaning, which are the heart of reading. Likewise, if teachers assume that children's second-language production directly reflects their comprehension, they are likely again to severely miscalculate children's reading abilities and capabilities. Research shows that phonological and even grammatical differences in second-language oral reading by non-native speakers of English do not always signal meaning or comprehension losses (Hudelson, 1981; Goodman & Goodman, 1978). Likewise, classroom observations reveal that second-language learners generally comprehend much more than they can produce orally or in writing. This means that neither pronunciation nor overall oral production in reading should be equated with a student's reading ability or comprehension, nor should they be allowed to become the focal point of instruction, especially when language-minority learners are involved.

If the language-minority child is in a reading program that includes native-language literacy instruction, how the reading process is conceptualized in that situation is also important. For example, one cannot assume that because of differences in codes (i.e., too different languages) the reading process will be different for the two languages, particularly if both languages are alphabetic and share some characteristics, as in the case of English and Spanish. Nor can one in turn assume that methods of reading instruction should differ with each language due to their differing surface features. In any language, reading can be viewed as a process of making sense of graphic symbols. The reader, regardless of the surface features of the code, approaches reading expecting to get meaning (Smith, 1978; Goodman, 1981). Miscue research studies of reading in several different languages show that learners across these languages apply similar strategies in dealing with print (Hudelson, 1981). Therefore, for reading programs in bilingual education, planners and practitioners would do well to focus children's attention on these universals in the reading process and should not infer that the learner faces radically different tasks in reading the two languages.

Developmental Aspects and Learner Differences

Reading-language professionals today are questioning the rigid and arbitrary manner in which the language arts—listening, speaking, reading, and writing—traditionally have been defined in the schools. What may be presented as separate, unrelated categories in the school curriculum may not necessarily be that in the learner's mind (Smith, 1979). Ample evidence of the highly interrelated and mutually reinforcing nature of the various aspects of language is provided by the reading-language behavior of many language-minority children.

In bilingual education programs, it is becoming clear that hard-and-fast rules cannot be imposed on children's language-literacy learning. It cannot be assumed, for example, that reading and writing will develop only after a defined, fixed level of second-language oral development. Evidence shows that oral language and literacy learning in a second language develop almost simultaneously or side by side (Goodman, Goodman & Flores, 1979; Hudelson & Barrera, in press). In fact, learners can expand their knowledge of the second language in contextualized, meaningful formats (Elley, 1981). Some learners may want to do second-language writing even before second-language reading. Then, too, we are becoming increasingly aware that children's second-language proficiency develops not only in the classroom but also away from it, obviously without the benefit of predetermined sequences of skills or drills such as those provided in the classroom. It seems that the oft-dis cussed notion of "transfer" in bilingual reading is essentially a moot topic. In many instances, children do not wait for the teacher to "transfer" them on the basis of some oral language test score or native-language reading level as is the practice in many bilingual education programs; transfer to second-language reading can be controlled by the learner. If second-language reading is seen as desirable, meaningful, and purposeful, it is likely and natural for the child to move from native-language literacy into second-language reading, without waiting on any externally-imposed criteria to signal that it can be done. Teachers in bilingual classrooms as well as monolingual English classrooms need to create for second-language learners an environment that encourages such transfer.

In all classrooms serving language-minority students, teachers need to be reminded that as second-language learners are growing in that language, it is unrealistic to expect their performance to measure up to a native English yardstick. Those language "mistakes" and "goofs" that children make during the course of second-language learning (Dulay & Burt, 1974) are as important to language growth as the "mistakes" that are made during first-language learning in infancy and early childhood (Black, 1980). Teachers need to understand that these are systematic and natural aspects of second-language learning. In oral reading of the second language, teachers need to be able to recognize dialectal and developmentally-based miscues and to know that they do not always interfere with comprehension. In testing and formal evaluation, standards and demands need to be adjusted in light of second-language learner's development. Any test intended for the native English-speaker or reader cannot fairly assess a learner's beginning proficiency in the second language. Above all, teachers must be encouraged to focus on the meaning of children's communication and messages and not on their form.

Finally, literacy learning in the second language will vary with the literacy background of the learner. If the learner is already literate to some degree in his native language, reading in the second language will not be a totally unfamiliar task simply because he already knows how to read. He is not faced with having to learn to read all over again, and, in fact, may be quite willing and able, not to mention eager, to tackle both oral language and literacy tasks simultaneously in the second language. In contrast, the student with no native-language reading experiences faces a more demanding task when confronted with second-language reading. That student has to learn what reading is all about.

Overall, to deal more effectively with second-language development, teachers would do well to heed two points. First, children's second-language learning, like all language learning, takes time to grow. And second, individual differences in second-language reading are to be expected and accepted as they are in all reading instruction.

SHIFTING TO ANOTHER PERSPECTIVE

All too often, reading instruction for the language-minority child is viewed from a remedial perspective, regardless of the instructional setting. What do I mean by this? Simply stated, the child is still looked upon as "deficient" in some respect (Dubois & Valdes, 1980), and reading instruction is provided largely as a "catch-up" or "patch-up" program. More than likely, the student is still measured by a native-English "yardstick," with linguistic and cultural differences seen as "problems" in the regular reading program, or even "congenital deficiencies" (Giordano, 1978). In some instances, the reading education of the language-minority child may be a continuing series of disjointed, unrelated, and even contradictory literacy experi-

65

ences, as the child is shuttled back and forth between the regular classroom and sundry special-assistance programs. I cannot state strongly enough that the language-minority child must be provided with a basic reading program that is comprehensive, coherent, and developmental in nature, not "remedial," "corrective," "transitional," or "special."

A Positive Outlook

To borrow some words from Ken Goodman (1979), we cannot lament that we "know nothing" about the teaching of reading to language-minority children; we "know more" today than ever before and this knowledge holds promise for strengthening reading programs for this school population. From all that we know, reading instruction—to be most effective and relevant for the language-minority learner—must be grounded in a positive view of the child and should strive to use the child's experiences and background knowledge as a "bridge" to school and book content. This does not mean that the child's world view should be the entire emphasis of the reading program, but it does mean that for facilitating certain aspects of reading development, this emphasis may be more effective than one that overlooks or looks down upon what the learner brings to the reading program (Au, 1980).

The importance of capitalizing on the learner's world knowledge has been supported repeatedly and in different ways by current reading-language literature. For example, some researchers have observed that text relating directly to the learner's own world and belief system consistently leads to higher levels of reading comprehension (Joag-dev and Steffensen, 1980; Goodman & Goodman, 1978). Furthermore, instructional strategies that integrate the child's past experiences with new reading matter induce greater learning and motivation (Au, 1979). Additionally, there is some evidence that the processing of text features such as story structure may be somewhat influenced by the reader's cultural background (McClure, Mason, & Williams, 1981; Goodman & Goodman, 1978). These findings suggest that the learner's background, if viewed positively, can be used to facilitate reading growth.

Assuring Quality

No one disputes the importance of reading skills to the individual's functioning in school and society. For that reason, the reading instruction we offer language-minority children cannot be marginal instruction.

If the reading program for any of these children begins with native-literacy instruction, then that instruction should be a full-bodied program, not merely a token component or one lacking some or many of the various resources that go into making a quality reading program. Overall, native-language reading instruction should be replete with literacy experiences that "make sense" to the reader, that is, they are seen as worthwhile, purposeful, meaningful, and interesting. Reading in the home language should be interrelated with and supported by the other language arts in that language. At the same time, native-language reading and second-language reading should be viewed as mutually reinforcing strands and not as disparate, competing spheres of instruction.

If reading instruction for the language-minority child is to be in English only, most of the foregoing also holds true. Language-minority children need quality English-as-a-second-language programs that are truly that—second-language programs—and not merely unchanged native-English programs imposed on them without the benefit of special strategies and activities that can accommodate their linguistic and cultural differences. The results of imposing such traditional, unmodified reading curricula on language-minority children are only too well-known.

66

In this era of accountability and nostalgia for the "basics," we must understand the needs of language-minority children well enough to avoid nourishing and perpetuating myopic attitudes about their reading education. To begin with, we must not allow the teaching of reading to these children to be reduced to simplistic, arbitrary, and predetermined lists or sequences of instructional experiences that do not add up to reading. The "whole" of language-literacy learning for bilingual and second-language learners cannot be reduced so simply. Furthermore, we should be careful not to apply to these children inappropriate and insensitive evaluation instruments that cannot validly measure their abilities and potential. Above all, we must not lose sight of, or compromise, quality as a necessary dimension of the reading education of language-minority children.

SUMMARY AND RECOMMENDATIONS

Having outlined what I see as essential to the planning and delivery of reading instruction for language-minority children, I now want to suggest what is required to transform these essentials into instructional realities in our increasingly diverse classrooms. Although I admit that the factors to be considered in working toward this goal are many and complex, there is one important and logical first step we must take if we are to move significantly toward enhancing the quality of reading instruction for language-minority children. Quite simply and assuredly, we must work to increase teachers' understanding, not just of pedagogy, but, more basically, of learning, specifically of how children grow in language and literacy. Within this plan of teacher education or retraining, there must be a deliberate effort to examine all the assumptions that teachers hold about the linguistic, cognitive, and social growth of language-minority children. Only by examining these assumptions against a backdrop of modern knowledge can we begin to make them more accurate, and perhaps move more easily toward translating them into appropriate and effective learning experiences. Others have pointed the way to similar directions (Goodman, Goodman & Flores, 1979; Lindfors, 1980).

We know that knowledgeable and understanding teachers do make a difference in children's learning to read; the key to more effective and relevant instruction is an enlightened teacher who knows and understands children and how they learn. We have a base of knowledge that can help us to build quality reading instruction for bilingual and second-language learners in our schools. We must now disseminate that knowledge to all teachers and school personnel who shape reading instruction for these children.

REFERENCES

Au, K. H. Using the experience-text-relationship method with minority children. *The Reading Teacher,* 1979, *32,* 677-679.

Au, K. H. Cultural congruence in the social organization of a reading lesson with Hawaiian students. Paper presented at the annual meeting of the American Educational Research Association, Boston, Mass., April 7-11, 1980. ED 193-600

Au, K. H. & Mason, J. M. Social organizational factors in learning to read: the balance of rights hypothesis. *Reading Research Quarterly,* 1981, *17,* 115-152.

Barrera, R. B. Bilingual reading in the primary grades: some questions about questionable views and practices. In T. H. Escobedo (Ed.) *Early Childhood - Bilingual Education: An Hispanic Perspective.* New York, N.Y.: Teachers College Press, in press.

Black, J. K. Those "mistakes" tell us a lot. *Language Arts,* 1980, *57*(3), 508-513.

Cazden, C. B. Social context of learning to read. In J. T. Guthrie (Ed.) *Comprehension and Teaching: Research Reviews.* Newark, Delaware: International Reading Association, 1981.

Dubois. B. L. & Valdes, G. Mexican-American child bilingualism: double deficit? *The Bilingual Review/La Revista Bilingue,* 1980, *7,* 1-7.

Dulay, H. C. & Burt, M. K. Errors and strategies in child second language acquisition. *TESOL Quarterly,* 1974, *8*(2), 129-136.

Elley, W. B. The role of reading in bilingual contexts. In J. T. Guthrie (Ed.) *Comprehension and Teaching: Research Reviews.* Newark, Delaware: International Reading Assocation, 1981.

Giordano, G. Commentary: "Congenetial verbal deficiency" in Navajo children—more on testing. *The Reading Teacher,* 1978, 32(2), 132-134.

Goodman, K. S. Reading: a psycholinguistic guessing game. In H. Singer & R. Ruddell (Eds.) *Theoretical Models and Processes of Reading.* Newark, Delaware: International Reading Association, 1976. (2nd edition)

Goodman, K. S. The know-more and the know-nothing movements in reading: a personal response. *Language Arts,* 1979, 56(6), 657-663.

Goodman, K. S. & Goodman, Y. Reading of American children whose language is a stable rural dialect of English and a language other than English. (Final report, Project NIE-00-3-0087). Washington, D.C.: U.S. Department of Education, 1978.

Goodman, K. S., Goodman, Y., & Flores, B. *Reading in the bilingual classroom: literacy and biliteracy.* Rosslyn, Virginia: National Clearinghouse for Bilingual Education, 1979.

Hudleson, S. (Ed.) *Learning to read in different languages.* (Language and Literacy Series: 1). Washington, D.C.: Center for Applied Linguistics, 1981.

Hudelson, S. & Barrera, R. B. Bilingual/second-language learners and reading. In L. W. Searfoss & J. W. Readence *(Helping Children Learn to Read.* Englewood Cliffs, N.J.: Prentice-Hall Publishers, Inc., in press.

Joag-dev, C. & Steffensen, M. S. Studies of the bicultural reader: implications for teachers and librarians. (Reading Education Report No. 12). Champaign, Illinois: Center for the Study of Reading, 1980.

Lindfors, J.W. *Children's language and learning. Englewood Cliffs, N.J.: Prentice-Hall Publishers, Inc., 1980.*

McClure, E., Mason, J., & Williams, J. *Sociocultural variables in children's sequencing of stories. (Technical Report No. 209). Champaign, Illinois: Center for the Study of Reading, 1981.*

Santa, C. M. *Children's reading comprehension: a final word.* In C. M. Santa & B. L. Hayes (Eds.) *Children's prose comprehension: research and practice.* Newark, Delaware: International Reading Association, 1981.

Smith, F. The language arts and the learner's mind. *Language Arts,* 1979, *56*(2), 118-125, 145.

Smith, F. *Understanding reading.* New York, N.Y.: Holt, Rinehart, and Winston, 1978. (2nd edition)

Steffensen, M. S., Joag-dev, C., & Anderson, R. C. A cross-cultural perspective on reading comprehension. *Reading Research Quarterly,* 1979, *15,* 10-29.

---

[1]In this paper, the term "language-minority" is used to refer to children who are of non-English language background and who have little or no proficiency in English. The term encompasses native-born bilingual children and non-native children for whom English is a second language.

PART V:
ORAL COMMUNICATION

ORAL COMMUNICATION INSTRUCTION:
GOALS AND TEACHER NEEDS

Barbara Lieb-Brilhart
National Institute of Education

During the early years of schooling in this country, the ability to speak articulately and persuasively was viewed as central to one's education (Wallace, 1954). However, the rise of silent reading in the nineteenth century and the emphasis on literature and composition helped foster a view of oral communication as "speech arts," reducing it to an elective or extracurricular activity in the English curriculum. Furthermore, early linguistic studies demonstrating that children learn the rules and structures of discourse before they enter kindergarten supported the view of some educators that speaking and listening are "naturally" learned acts which require no further intervention from the school. The few educators who continued to view oral communication as "basic" for all students split off from the English teachers in 1914 and continued to promote research and instruction in oral communication. Unfortunately, this split contributed to the increasing twentieth-century fragmentation of language and communication instruction. Only recently have we begun to "put humpty-dumpty together again," to recognize interrelationships between oral and written communication and the need for basic instruction in both these skills at every age level and in every discipline.

Before we explore the goals of oral communication instruction and the knowledge and abilities teachers need to fulfill them, we should recognize that the field of oral communication did not stand still between its relegation to elective status and its current recognition as a basic skill. During this time the field of speech communication expanded the ancient discipline of rhetoric to incorporate research from the behavioral and social sciences. Today, most colleges and universities offer a variety of programs emphasizing interpersonal, organizational, public, and mass communication. But concepts such as the importance of the receiver in communication, the interactive nature of the speaking/listening process, and the role of nonverbal communication in the interactive process—all of which have shaped communication instruction in post-secondary education for at least three decades—have only recently begun to filter down to elementary and secondary school instruction. Although some of us still remember high school speech contests with nostalgia, we should remember that as more is learned about the contexts, there is less enthusiasm for speech as a behavior to be rehearsed for the winning of trophies (Del Polito and Lieb-Brilhart, 1981).

Within this changing framework for oral communication instruction, Wood (1981) predicts that the 1980s will see (1) a shift away from the development of literacy skills (reading and writing) to the development of communication skills (including speaking and listening); (2) a stress on functional approaches which emphasize student needs to participate successfully in peer, family and classroom situations; and (3) more student talk during instruction "so that the classroom will become an alive, talkative and sometimes chaotic environment" (p.13).

Thus we have come full circle to the renewed recognition or oral communication as a basic skill. However, this time we can offer instruction that rests on a better base of knowledge about communication processes and about the development of children. In the remainder of this paper I will discuss the parameters of oral communication instruction, its role as a basic skill, and the related needs for teacher education.

Parameters of Oral Communication Instruction

In 1978 the Speech Communication Association (SCA) and the American Speech-Language-Hearing Association (ASHA) published their *Standards for Effective Oral Communication Instruction*. The definition of oral communication in this document helps define the parameters for instruction:

Oral Communication: the process of interacting through heard and spoken messages in a variety of situations. Effective oral communication is a learned behavior, involving the following processes:

1. Speaking in a variety of educational and social situations: Speaking involves, but is not limited to, arranging and producing messages through the use of voice, articulation, vocabulary, syntax and nonverbal cues (e.g., gesture, facial expression, vocal cues) appropriate to the speaker and listeners.
2. Listening in a variety of educational and social situations: Listening involves, but is not limited to, hearing, perceiving, discriminating, interpreting, synthesizing, evaluating, organizing and remembering information from verbal and nonverbal messages.

This definition stresses *interaction*, as does much current instruction. Attention has shifted toward interaction in everyday conversations as well as in public discourse where a speaker dominates while others listen. Contemporary models depict communication as a transactional process wherein individuals exchange roles as speakers and listeners in the course of interacting. Such models refute previous notions of public speaking as "monologue." Speakers continuously adjust messages based on nonverbal or verbal cues from listeners; listeners simultaneously encode and transmit nonverbal feedback as they receive, interpret and evaluate meanings from speakers.

The definition also emphasizes the notion of communication as a *learned* behavior. It is well understood that we speak the speech that we have heard in childhood. What is less understood is the extent to which communication is possible if there is interference in the natural stages of development. For example, there is the recent case of the abused child, Genie, who, after having been isolated and deprived of interaction until age 13, received extensive help from various professionals in learning how to communicate. Although she learned to function well on tasks governed by the right brain hemisphere (e.g., visual and tactile orientation and holistic thinking), she made poor progress on tasks governed by the left hemisphere (e.g., syntactic rules, auditory memory and abstract thinking). This case (Curtiss, 1977) and other evidence support the belief that there are critical periods of development for many of the processes that govern speech and communication.

We know that speaking and listening, unlike reading and writing, are biological heritages. As long as the child's development is normal and there are communicative human beings in the environment, the child will learn to speak. However, these facts about speech learning have confused educators' perceptions of what needs to be taught under the rubric of oral communication. Many ask what remains to be taught if, by the time they come to school, children know most of the sounds of their language, a vocabulary of about 2,000 words, basic syntax, and verbal and nonverbal meanings. The answer lies in what we now know about communication development and adult communication needs.

Oral communication instruction must expand students' repertoires of skills so that they can communicate effectively in diverse contexts (Allen and Brown, 1976). In other words, the child's ability to communicate in diverse contexts requires a repertoire of functional skills and expansion of the skills that are developed in the early years.

The SCA/ASHA definition of oral communication also includes the notion of interaction in a *variety of situations*. The *Standards* describe the need for instruction to develop communication skills appropriate for a range of *situations* (e.g., informal to formal); a range of *purposes* (e.g., informing, persuading, sharing feelings); a range of *audiences* (e.g., classmates, teachers, family, employers); a range of communication *forms* (e.g., conversation, group discussion, public speaking); and a range of speaking *styles* (e.g., impromptu, extemporaneous, reading from manuscript).

Oral communication instruction, then, seeks to build on children's accomplishments in language and communication from the time they enter school. There are six areas in which skills must be developed:

VERBAL SKILLS: This area encompasses those skills involved in producing and responding to oral language (including production and discrimination of sounds, production and comprehension of sentence structures, fluency and elaboration of utterances, and production and response to figurative language). In summarizing the phases in children's development of meanings, Wood (1981) describes the last phase, which continues throughout the school years. Children learn during this phase to select from among many possible meanings the one meaning that fits the context at any given moment. They also learn "scripts" or appropriate modes of communication for various social contexts, such as the rules of dinner table talk and patterns of behavior for the "good guys" and the "bad guys" on television.

NONVERBAL SKILLS: Just as verbal behavior is culturally learned as we interact with others, so is nonverbal behavior. Studies of kinesics (gestures, stance, facial expression and other bodily movement), indicate that some of the earliest communication of the child is through body motion—pointing, gesturing and movements of the whole body (Wood, 1981). Other studies show that the use of body movements for communication improves with maturation (Dittman, 1972). The child also learns to use distances (proxemics) appropriate to conversation, with the adult norm stabilizing at about third grade (Knapp, 1978). Vocal behavior as a part of nonverbal communication develops in infancy, but during the elementary school years, children develop intonation patterns that support the more complex syntactic structures they are learning. However, because nonverbal communication carries most of the meaning in interpersonal communication, and because it is a critical factor in intercultural communication, children and adults need continuous help in learning to convey and to comprehend vocal, proxemic and kinesic cues.

INTERACTION SKILLS: In this area, children must learn the specific skills for maintaining dialogue. For example, they must learn to speak relevantly to the context and to monitor an appropriate quantity of speech. Other interaction skills are equally important: turn taking in conversation, continuity in maintaining one's own viewpoint, sending and responding to feedback, and so on.

CRITICAL/EVALUATIVE SKILLS: Children must also learn to be critical and to evaluate spoken messages. Such skills include distinguishing fact from opinion, judging the biases and qualifications of speakers, judging logic and consistency among reasons, and accurately interpreting moods, sarcasm, irony, etc.

MESSAGE STRATEGY SKILLS: There are many skills involved in developing and comprehending whole pieces of discourse; these include constructing main ideas, developing supporting ideas (e.g., analogies, examples and statistical data), developing arguments and evidence, and using psychological appeals. Traditional instruction in language arts probably has paid more attention to these skills in written, rather than oral, communication; however, those students who elect speech in secondary school programs are apt to focus heavily on message strategy skills.

FUNCTIONAL/SITUATIONAL SKILLS: These skills involve the use of verbal and nonverbal language to accomplish specific purposes in various situations. Such skills are based on appropriate adaptation of messages to the knowledge and experiences of others at specific times and places. When people violate cultural rituals (e.g., dozing at important meetings, terminating a phone conversation without saying "goodbye") or when they do not seem to understand what kind of communication is required of them in specific situations, we either think them odd or look for "hidden messages." Children and many adults need to be taught about the impact their messages have on others, and they need to develop ways to communicate appropriately in diverse situations.

To work in any of the six skill areas described above, the child must learn to take the perspective of another person. Piaget's work set the stage for a view of communication development as a decentering process; speech that is initially "egocentric" gradually becomes social. And research establishes the development of social speech, showing that children's persuasive strategies become increasingly sophisticated with age. For example, Delia, Kline and Burleson (1979) demonstrate that as children mature, they become better at using reasons and adapting their messags to listeners in order to persuade them. Young children make unelaborated requests when persuading: "Could I have a party please?" Older children might say, "I've never had anything like this before, so why can't you let me have a party?" A still older child tries to anticipate counter arguments: "There wouldn't be a lot of running around, and there would only be about five people." At the highest level of complexity, the child takes the listener's perspective in articulating an advantage: "I know that you like to meet my friends, and a party would be a great way to do this."

Children display wide variations in their abilities to perform in the six skill areas, especially those directly related to taking the perspective of the other person. In the extreme case, children labeled "learning disabled" may be unable to interpret and respond appropriately to social cues in the course of interaction. Often problems in communication are more debilitating to the child and disruptive to the classroom than problems in other academic areas. Bader (1975), in summarizing the research in social perception and learning disabilities, notes that "learning disabled" children often try too hard to say the right thing, speak too loudly, interrupt frequently, get too close when they talk, and miss subtleties of meaning.

Another serious developmental problem in communication is "communication apprehension," sometimes called "reticence" or "shyness." Communication apprehension is a broader problem than stage fright, since it usually involves not only a fear of public speaking, but of conversational, informal speaking as well. Evidence shows that between ten and twenty percent of college students and adults suffer from this problem, but percentages are likely to be somewhat higher in secondary and elementary schools (Hurt, Scott, McCroskey, 1978). Some indicators of communication apprehension in the classroom are using a low voice, sitting at the back of the room or in an area of least interaction, making poor eye contact, and refusing to communicate in class. Highly apprehensive students have negative attitudes toward school (Hurt and Preiss, 1978) and may be low achievers (McCroskey, 1977).

Several remedial approaches to communication apprehension are available (Phillips, 1977; McCroskey, 1977), but these are too complex to describe here. It is vital, however, that teachers be educated to recognize the problems of the communication disabled and to learn ways to help them in the classroom. One simple practice is to stop forcing apprehensive students to stand in front of their classmates in order to communicate. Easing students from informal, dyadic exercises into the more formal situations helps lessen apprehension. In the case of the learning disabled, inabilities to interpret nonverbal cues and to interact appropriately should be recognized and treated developmentally, just as difficulties with math or reading are.

Oral Communication as a Basic Skill

There are three overall goals for communication instruction:
(1) to ensure that students learn speaking, listening and interactive skills that enhance learning at all levels of education, regardless of the content studied;
(2) to ensure that students understand and can use communication principles that will help them in their relationships with family, peers, community groups, and in other social contexts;
(3) to ensure that students understand and can use communication principles that will help them at work. The goals, then, are to help students communicate effectively in academic, social and work contexts.

In the academic context, students who are effective in oral communication have a better chance for success than those who are not. There are several reasons for this, the most obvious being that teaching/learning is essentially a communication process. For example, Friedrich (1980), after examining research on classroom variables, concluded that the quality of communication may account for twenty-five percent of the achievement variance in the classroom. Others have pointed out that most classroom time is spent in talk (Bellack, 1966; Flanders, 1970; *Language for Life,* 1975). In addition, oral communication is vital to achievement in other basic skill areas. According to the *Essentials of Education Statement* (1981), endorsed by a number of professional associations, symbolic behavior is at the core of all other learning. Oral communication (our first encounter with symbolic behavior) is the base upon which all other skills develop.

In the area of social relationships, we know experientially that oral communication skills contribute to the maintenance of stable human relationships. The demand for assertiveness training, family communication workshops, parent effectiveness training, and marital communication attest to the value of empathic listening, direct and open communication, ownership of feelings, feedback, and other concepts taught under the rubric of interpersonal communication. A panel meeting in 1973 to define social competency in young children included the following in its statement of goals: sensitivity and understanding in social relationships; positive and affectionate personal relationships; critical thinking skills; problem solving skills; and enjoyment of humor, play and fantasy (Anderson and Messick, 1973). Oral communication instruction can contribute directly to these goals or social competence.

Success in the world of work is also dependent upon oral communication skills. For example, Lockwood and Boatman (1975) and Hanna (1978) found that representatives from a variety of businesses and professions saw the following communication skills as important in their work: interviewing, group problem solving, listening, motivating people, persuading, giving directions, questioning, speaking publicly, and building relationships. In his summary of studies indicating the need for oral communication in the world of work, Wolvin (1981) reported that M.B.A. graduates ranked persuasiveness as the most important skill in business and that engineers ranked speech communication as fourth among 123 areas required for their work.

In discussing the goals of oral communication instruction, we must emphasize that it is not enough merely to increase the amount of classroom talk or to feel satisfied that talking is used in pre-writing or in reading aloud. To the horror of the speech specialist, teachers may feel that they have integrated instruction when students write out or memorize oral discourse. What is needed is a sound program of oral communication instruction which recognizes the overlap and interrelatedness with written communication, but which permits separate time for each kind of instruction.

73

Recent research, particularly that of Kroll (1981), indicates that a child's oral and written discourse become increasingly similar in content, but dissimilar in approach, as the child matures. Kantor and Rubin (1981) conceptualize three facets of differentiation in oral and written communication: *Social Awareness* involves intention to affect and be affected by others; in writing, the individual must "fictionalize" an audience, while in speaking, the audience's concrete presence "renders the work of inferring audience demands less taxing." *Coding* involves control over larger chunks of discourse and knowledge of language pragmatics; while formal speech shares aspects of written coding (writers provide context information and include all necessary information), every-day speech tolerates implicit meanings, incomplete details and capitalizes on an immediate shared context. *Reconstruction of Experience* involves the ways in which we relate our perceptions of the world and the manipulation of symbols; speech fades fast and is less planned, therefore facilitating cognition differently from writing, which can leave a permanent trace and is subject to revision. Writing allows for more reflection, while speaking allows for more complex social perspective-taking.

Thus, while there are areas for interrelating instruction in oral and written communication, each embodies some skills which must be learned and developed separately.

Teacher Needs

Because of the elective status of speech in the secondary schools, the responsibility for teaching oral communication has often fallen on teachers who offer poor instruction because of inadequate academic preparation, lack of interest, or lack of time. With shrinking education budgets, there is little hope that districts will hire speech communication teachers, even though the pay-off would be worth the investment. However, the Speech Communication Association and the American Theatre Association have jointly prepared guidelines to assist those districts who wish to hire or up-grade elementary and secondary school communication specialists (*Preparation of Elementary and Secondary Teachers in Speech Communication and Theatre,* 1978).

A second approach, which may have the best long-term impact, is to exploit the abilities of all teachers to teach communication skills. This approach involves two aspects: the first focuses on the student (i.e., the teacher's knowledge of oral communication development and the provision for instructional opportunities); the second focuses on the development of the teacher's own communication skills. The two aspects are interrelated, since the modeling of functional communication by the teacher influences the student's communication development.

The first aspect includes several generic competencies described in the SCA/ATA model of competencies for non-specialists in communication. These include the following: (1) identifying stages and factors in language and communication development; (2) interrelating reading, writing, speaking and listening, and functional communication; (3) coping with communication problems of students; (4) enhancing communication development through instructional activities; (5) fostering expression of and receptiveness toward divergent viewpoints and communication styles. All these skills are needed for the teacher confronted with the diversity of the mainstreamed, multicultural classroom.

Just as students must develop communication oriented toward the "perspective of the other," so must teachers prepare and deliver messages appropriate to a wide range of students and instructional contexts. Teachers must organize content from the framework of their students, use language that is appropriate to the ages, experiences and developmental levels of students, be aware of the impact of nonverbal behavior in communicating attitudes and values, and be receptive to divergent viewpoints and ways of speaking. The emerging research on classroom climate indicates that teachers' responses are important in creating non-threatening environments conducive to achievement (Seiler, Lieb-Brilhart, and Schuelke, in press). While communication instruction for teachers is increasing rapidly (Lynn, 1976), much more is needed.

To meet the needs of teachers, pre-service institutions should require communication education for all prospective teachers. Moreover, we need support for approaches like those used in the National Writing Project. Such approaches could provide in-service instruction focusing on the teachers' communication skills as the key to developing students' communication skills.

Recommendations and Summary

1. *A national (and, perhaps, international), conference of communication education specialists, socio-linguists, and language arts specialists should meet to examine the status of and need for research in oral communication and to suggest implications for instruction.*

The work of socio-linguists and communication specialists is moving toward common viewpoints embodied in functional approaches. The socio-linguist's research on language development should be integrated with the communication specialists's long history and experiential base in instruction and intervention in oral communication processes.

2. *Schools must emphasize instructional planning which allows time for oral communication instruction, not only in support of other language instruction, but for its own sake as well.*

Adequate time must be allowed for oral communication in the six skill areas outlined in this paper. There must be clear goals in the curriculum, as there are for other subject areas, and not just activities which support other language arts.

3. *Schools should provide speech communication specialists as consultants to other teachers to help them develop their own communication skills and the skills of their pupils.*

Specialists might work as teacher/consultants to help with the teacher's communication needs or to suggest ways of coping with the communication-disabled child.

4. *A nationwide effort such as that undertaken for the National Writing Project should be undertaken for a national oral communication project.*

The National Writing Project, which, since 1974, has supported several thousand high school and college teachers, has received acclaim from educators and the public for its impact on students' writing skills (McCarthy, November 17, 1981). Efforts to support oral communication teachers must help teachers improve their own skills and those of their colleagues and students.

5. *Pre-service and inservice education in oral communication must be provided for teachers and administrators so that schools can intervene effectively in communication development.*

Oral communication instruction should be required for teacher certification in every state; such instruction may take the form of a course, but should be incorporated continuously throughout the teacher education sequence, including the practicum.

Including oral communication among the "basics" gives us an opportunity to integrate instruction in the various language and communication skills. By doing this we can stress the shared concerns as well as the uniqueness of each essential communication skill. We can also find ways of improving instruction in *all* areas by stressing the essence of the teaching/learning process, which consists primarily of speaking and listening in an interactive mode.*

*This paper is based primarily on work completed during the writer's previous position as Associate Executive Secretary of the Speech Communication Association and as a continuing member of that organization. The work was not sponsored by the National Institute of Education and does not necessarily represent the views of that agency.

REFERENCES

Allen, R.R., and Brown, K.L. *Developing Communication Competence in Children.* Skokie, IL: National Textbook Co., 1976.

Anderson, S. and Messick, S. *Social Competency in Young Children.* Princeton, NJ: Educational Testing Service, March 1973. ERIC Document No. 082 812.

Bader, B.W. *Social Perception and Learning Disabilities.* Des Moines, IA: Moon Lithographing, 1975.

Bellack, A.A., Kliebard, H.M., Hyman, R., and Smith, F.L. *The Language of the Classroom.* New York: Teachers College Press, 1966.

Curtiss, S.V. Genie: *A Psycholinguistic Study of a Modern-day Wild Child.* New York: Academic Press, 1977.

Delia, J.G., Kline, S.L., and Burleson, B.R. "The Development of Persuasive Communication Strategies in Kindergartners Through Twelfth Graders." *Communication Monographs,* 1979, *46,* 241-257.

Del Polito, C.M. and Lieb-Brilhart, B. "Implications of Oral Communication as a Basic Skill." In G.W. Friedrich (Ed.), *Education in the 80s: Speech Communication.* National Education Association of the United States, 1981, 123-129.

Dittman, A.T. "Development of Factors in Conversational Behavior." *Journal of Communication.* 1972, *22,* 404-423.

The Essentials of Education Statement. In A.C. Purves, "The Essentials of Education: An Overview." In L.Y. Mercier (Ed.), *The Essentials Approach: Rethinking the Curriculum for the 80s.* U.S. Department of Education, Basic Skills Improvement Program, September, 1981, 3-5.

Flanders, N.A. *Analyzing Teacher Behavior.* Reading, MA: Addison-Wesley, 1970.

Friedrich, G.W. "Effects of Teacher Behavior on the Acquisition of Communication Competencies." Unpublished paper presented at the AERA Convention, Toronto, Canada, 1978.

Hanna, M.S. "Speech Communication Training Needs in the Business Community." *Central States Speech Journal,* 29, 1978, 163-172.

Hurt, H.T. and Preiss, R. "Silence Isn't Necessarily Golden: Communication, Apprehension, Desired Social Choice, and Academic Success Among Middle-school Students. *Human Communication Research.* Summer 1978, 4, 315-328.

Kantor, K.J. and Rubin, D.L., "Between Speaking and Writing: Processes of Differentiation." In Kroll, B.M. and Vann, R.J., (Eds.) *Exploring Speaking-Writing Relationships:' Connections and Contrasts.* Urbana, IL: National Council of Teachers of English, 1981, Chapter 3.

Kroll, B.M., "Developmental Relationships Between Speaking and Writing." In Kroll, B.M. and Vann, R.J. (Eds) *Exploring Speaking-Writing Relationships: Connections and Contrasts.* Urbana, IL: National Council of Teachers of English, 1981, Chapter 2.

Language for Life: Report of the Committee of Inquiry Appointed by the Secretary of State for Education and Science. London: Her Majesty's Stationery Office, 1975.

Lockwood, D. and Boatman, S. "Marketability: Who Needs Us and What Can We Do for Them?" Unpublished paper presented at the Central States Speech Association Convention, Kansas City, Missouri, 1975.

Lynn, E.M. *Improving Classroom Communication: Speech Communication Instruction for Teachers.* Annandale, VA: Speech Communication Association and the ERIC Clearinghouse on Reading and Communication Skills, 1976.

McCarthy, Colman, "Who's Killing English?" *The Washington Post,* Tuesday, November, 17, 1981.

McCroskey, J.C., "Classroom Consequences of Communication Apprehension." *Communication Education,* January 1977, 26, 27-33.

Phillips, G.M., Rhetoritheraphy Versus the Medical Model: Dealing with Reticence. *Communication Education,* January 1977, 26, 34-43.

Preparation of Elementary and Secondary Teachers in Speech Communication and Theatre: Competency Models and Program Guidelines Recommended by the Speech Communication Association and the American Theatre Association. Annadale, VA: Speech Communication Assoc., 1978.

Seiler, W., Schuelke, D. and Lieb-Brilhart, B., *Communication in the Contemporary Classroom,* New York: Holt, Rinehart, Winston, 1982 (in press).

Shuy, R.W., "Learning to Talk Like Teachers." *Language Arts,* February, 1981, 58, 168-174.

Wallace, K.R., ed., *History of Speech Education in America,* New York: Appelton-Century-Crofts, Inc., 1954.

Wolvin, A.D., "Speech Communication in Applied Settings." In G.W. Friedrich (Ed.), *Education in the 80s: Speech Communication,* National Education Association of the United States, 1981, 42-49.

Wood, B.S. "Speech Communication in the Elementary School." In G.W. Friedrich (Ed.), *Education in the 80s: Speech Communication,* National Education Association of the United States, 1981, 13-13-21.

Wood, B.S., *Children and Communication: Verbal and Nonverbal Language Development.* Englewood Cliffs, NJ: Prentice Hall, 1981.

TEACHING AND ASSESSING ORAL COMMUNICATION

Kenneth L. Brown

University of Massachusetts

When a state or local education agency decides to include oral communication in its basic skills program, it faces three tasks: deciding which skills to teach, developing curricula for teaching the skills, and developing means of assessing them. In her paper, Dr. Lieb-Brilhart discussed oral communication skills that deserve attention in the schools; my focus is on teaching and assessing those skills.

Three years ago, just five states included speaking and listening in their basic learning skills programs (Brown, et al, 1979; Pipho, 1978, 1979), and most of those states had progressed no further than identifying skills to be taught. Today, however, thirty-three states are in various stages of including oral communication in their basic skills programs (Backlund, et al., in press). These stages range from *planning* to develop programs to *implementing* programs that have already been developed. So in three years we have seen increased activity in oral communication programs. But this activity has raised questions: What are the focuses of instruction? How should instruction be sequenced? Is direct intervention effective? How can the school and home cooperate? And how does one assess oral communication skills? I propose to address these questions by identifying current promising practices, noting problems, and recommending actions for extending the range of promising practices in the future.

Approaches to Instruction

A review of communication education literature and observations of classroom practices (Brown, et al., 1981) reveal five major approaches to instruction in oral communication. These approaches focus on component skills, communication activities, participant networks, referential communication games, and functional communication.

With the *component skills* approach, the teacher focuses attention on mastery of clusters of specific skills. Students usually concentrate on one set of skills at a time. For example, at one time they might concentrate on language skills such as building sentences, using words correctly, speaking grammatically, and demonstrating word knowledge. At another they might concentrate on organizational skills such as formulating central ideas, selecting and arranging supporting ideas, or outlining ideas. Other skills might cluster around delivery, audience analysis, nonverbal language, listening comprehension, and critical listening. Generally the method for teaching these skills involves concentrated practice, sometimes drill, until the particular skills are mastered. Skills may eventually be applied in practical communication situations, but for the sake of systematic development, they are first learned separately. Examples of the component skills approach appear in numerous language arts textbooks as well as in books by Byrne (1965), Haynes (1973), Lundsteen (1979), and Russell and Russell (1979).

The goal of the *communication activities* approach is to have students experience a variety of oral communication activities that presumably prepare them to engage in everyday situations. Typical elementary school activities are storytelling, conversation, discussion, reading aloud, listening games, creative dramatics, and giving talks. Secondary school activities include public speaking, small group discussion, oral interpretation of literature, debate, dramatics and radio-television speaking.

Because successful performance in each of these activities requires proficiency in many speaking and listening skills, a number of different skills are taught and assessed simultaneously. But the skills learned vary from one activity to another. This approach is commonly used by classroom specialists in speech as well as by non-specialists. The latter incorporate selected activities to motivate students and enrich learning in different areas of the curriculum. Elementary school materials that reflect the activities approach are Carlson (1970), Chambers (1970), Duke (1974), Erlich (1974), Glaus (1965), Henry (1967), and Mackintosh (1964); secondary school materials are Bacon (1974), Beyer, Lee and Wilkinson (1975), Braden (1972), Carlile (1972), Newcombe (1980), and Prentice, Pollard and McComas (1979).

While the component skills and activities approaches have been used for some time, the remaining three approaches are more recent. Through the *participant network* approach, skills are acquired through systematic instruction in interpersonal, small group, public, and mass communication. In this continuum, communication is differentiated by the number of persons communicating. Attention centers on the effect of speaker-listener distancing on interaction. Students develop skills appropriate to situations that range from spontaneous, informal and reciprocal interaction to rehearsed, formal and mediated communication. Emphasized in the secondary more than the elementary school, this approach stresses cognitive and affective learning as well as oral communication performance. Some sources that reflect this approach are Allen, et al., (1974), Allen, et al., (1976), Barbour and Goldberg (1974), Book and Galvin (1975), Brooks and Friedrich (1973), Galvin and Book (1981), Fletcher and Surlin (1978), and Newcombe and Robinson (1975).

The fourth approach, *referential communication games,* stresses interactive communication. One person (a speaker) attempts to communicate with another person (a listener) about a target object (a referent) in a set of alternatives. The speaker tries to inform the listener with accuracy and efficiency, while the listener aims to demonstrate comprehension in a goal-directed task. To be sure that students rely solely on verbal means of communication, the participants may not see each other; they either sit back-to-back or communicate across a table with a screen between them. Typical communication tasks include explaining how to assemble a model from blocks, how to select one picture out of a set of similar pictures, or how to find a destination on a map. Thus, this approach emphasizes constructing and comprehending verbal descriptions, explanations and directions. Since children take turns as speaker and listener, they practice both roles. The approach, which relies heavily on modeling, peer interaction, and feedback to improve communication quality, was derived from a research strategy (Fishbein and Osborne, 1971; Glucksberg, et al., 1975; Glucksberg, et al, 1966; Krauss and Glucksberg, 1969; Higgins, 1973; Lieb-Brilhart, 1965; Johnson, 1974), and has been adapted more recently for use in the classroom (Dickson, 1981; Dickson and Patterson, 1981; Gleason, 1972; and Mc-Caffrey, 1980).

The *functional communication* approach assumes that competent communication results from a wide range of communication skills and behaviors that are used appropriately and effectively. Instruction focuses on using language for five major functions. The informing function includes producing and comprehending informative messages by demonstrating, explaining, asking and answering questions, and instructing. The controlling function includes persuading, arguing, bargaining, suggesting, and demanding. The feeling function involves sharing one's feelings and reacting to others' feelings through acts such as exclaiming, commiserating, blaming, or apologizing. The imagining function taps ability to use language creatively in order to fantasize, speculate, tell tales, role-play, or dramatize. And the ritualizing function involves maintaining social relationships through acts such as greeting others, taking leave, taking turns, playing verbal games, and handling introductions. These functions are based on research conducted by Wells (1973), but Halliday (1977) and Tough (1977) provide other functional schemes. Experience with each of the five major functions is gained through exercises, simulations and problem situations created by the teacher and students. The situations are designed to help students (a) develop a wide repertoire of communication strategies and skills, (b) select skills which seem appropriate to the situations, (c) implement the skills through practice, and (d) evaluate the effectiveness and appropriateness of the skills employed. Allen and Brown (1976), Allen and Wood (1978), Book (1978), Glenn (1978), and Wood (1977a and b; 1981) provide numerous examples of this approach both for the elementary and secondary school levels.

Some of the above approaches are limited. For example, the component skills approach makes it possible to develop skills systematically, but when used alone, students may not learn when to employ those skills for functional effectiveness (Cazden, 1972). The activities approach affords opportunities for using many skills simultaneously and for integrating oral communication with other skills and curriculum areas, but some activities bear little resemblance to communication situations encountered outside the classroom.

Teachers and curriculum planners must decide whether to focus attention on discrete skills or on skills used for a purpose in a realistic context. They must also decide what approaches to employ to develop those skills. One approach need not be used exclusively. In fact, if the component skills approach is used, it ought to be combined with another approach such as functional communication. Examples of combining approaches are found in Staton-Spicer and Bassett (1980) and the State of Illinois (1981a).

Of the approaches I have outlined, teachers seem to employ the component skills and activities approaches most often. The referential and functional communication approaches are potentially the most useful, but educators are not as aware of them. Just as we want children to develop a range of skills, teachers need to expand their instructional options. They should become familiar with the different approaches to teaching oral communication, the assumptions about learning and communication that undergird each approach, the methods and materials of each approach, and the ways of combining approaches to produce desired results. In addition, they should be encouraged to experiment with those approaches that facilitate development of skills for purposeful communication.

Sequencing Instruction

Despite the proliferation of "pre-packaged" materials that sequence oral communication skills, I am unable to say, "Here is *the* sequence you should follow." Some efforts to sequence instruction have been based on taxonomies of educational objectives in the cognitive (Bloom, et al., 1956) and affective (Krathwohl, et al., 1964) domains (for example, see Lundsteen, 1979). Other sequences progress from small to larger units of discourse, from simple to complex tasks (McCaffrey, 1980; Project Signals, 1981; State of Illinois, 1981a), and from interpersonal to mass communication (Allen, et al., 1974; Galvin and Book, 1981; State of Illinois, 1981a). One of the best known sequences, Moffett's student-centered language arts curriculum (1968a and b), is based on a theory of discourse that increases the distance between speaker and audience and that moves students from perception of what is happening (drama), through narration of what happened, to generalizing what happens, to theorizing about what may happen.

Research has shed much light on the development of language, but future efforts at sequencing instruction will rest on a better understanding of the development of children's ability to *use* language for social purposes. Delia, et al., (1979), Dickson (1981), Ervin-Tripp and Mitchell-Kernan (1977), Halliday (1977), and Tough (1977) are notable examples of research that describes children's development of functional communication. Allen and Brown (1976), Cazden (1972), Dickson and Patterson (1981), Wood (1981), Hopper and Naremore (1978), Lindfors (1980), and McCaffrey (1980) suggest how curricula can be constructed to complement that development.

In the absence of a definitive instructional sequence, teachers should become familiar with what is known about children's developmental course in oral communication. Knowing that course and recognizing individual variations within it will help one to provide instruction that moves the child increasingly toward explicitness of speech, verbal and ideational fluency, sensitivity to the responses of others, adaptation of message to audience, flexibility in attempting alternative strategies and encodings, talk about topics of mutual interest, and self-monitoring of communicative effectiveness and appropriateness.

Effects of Intervention

Teachers may employ different kinds of intervention to develop communication skills. When they merely incorporate oral communication experiences in classrooms, usually in the context of some other subject or unit of study, or when they comment occasionally on a student's speaking or listening effectiveness, they rely on informal instruction, that is, on direct intervention. In this case, developing oral communication skills is incidental to developing skills or knowledge in some other content area.

Direct intervention involves identifying oral communication skills that need to be taught, providing instructional methods and materials to develop those skills, and evaluating results. Instructional methods employed may be either more or less didactic. More didactic methods include telling students how to communicate in a given situation and critiquing their efforts. Less didactic methods include having students interact with models, using sequenced materials to facilitate the development of skills, reversing speaker and listener roles, and providing feedback through questioning. Whether more or less didactic methods are employed, intervention is direct when it seeks to modify a targeted set of skills through planned means.

Studies indicate that direct intervention results in improved communicative performance (Asher and Wigfield, 1981; McCaffrey, 1980; Patterson and Kister, 1981; Shantz, 1981; Whitehurst and Sonnenschein, 1981; also see Brown, 1976, for a review of fifteen earlier studies). Children improve in message fluency, in efficiency and organization, in cognitive perspective-taking, in eliciting and responding to feedback, and in using verbal language to describe, explain, and give directions. In addition, improvement continues after instruction, providing chidren have additional opportunities for using these skills. But students have difficulty transferring skills learned in one context (e.g., a descriptive task) to a different context (e.g., a persuasive task). This suggests that skills need to be taught in different contexts.

As a basic skill, oral communication must be interrelated with other skills. Informal instruction affords opportunity for practice and reinforcement of a variety of oral communication skills, but direct intervention is necessary when children lack specific skills needed for effective communication. When planning and implementing direct intervention programs, teachers and administrators should (1) identify clearly the skills to be taught; (2) engage students in interaction with models and peers; (3) employ functional tasks where students construct and respond to messages for specific purposes; (4) provide ample opportunity for practice; and (5) stress feedback that makes the student aware of message adequacies and inadequacies.

Home-School Cooperation

Parents are the child's first teachers of oral communication, though they are not always aware of this important role. The family influences the child's acquisition of language, the child's style and form of speech, and the child's confidence and willingness to talk and listen.

Because oral communication skills are strongly influenced by the home environment, basic skills programs conducted in the schools should assist parents to contribute positively to their children's oral communication development. Project Signals (Barclift, et al., 1980) and the State of Illinois (1981b) extend their communication programs beyond the classroom by offering resource materials that describe the parent's role in promoting communication development, games and activities for use at home, and available references on parent-child communication. Home-school cooperation can occur in other ways, such as offering parent seminars on the acquisition and development of communication, with emphasis on the parent's role in providing a rich, but calm and pressure-free communication environment; developing a library of resources on parent-child communication; and including parents in committees that plan the school's oral communication curriculum.

Assessing Oral Communication Skills

Loban (1976) suggests that a reason for the neglect of oral language instruction is the absence of oral language testing in the schools. Some educators see assessment of oral communication as based on "soft" data. By this, they mean oral communication is not assessed by a standardized, machine scored, multiple choice test.

At least three studies completed in the past four years (Brown, et al., 1979; Larson, et al., 1978; Rubin, et al., in prep.) have reviewed over one hundred instruments that assess different aspects of oral communication. There is no paucity of measures and no aspect of functional communication for which measurement problems are prohibitive (Larson, et al., 1978). But existing instruments do present problems for evaluating oral communication performance in the context of large-scale basic skills assessment. Rubin et al. (in prep.) review these problems in more depth than space permits here, but a few will be mentioned. First, there is considerable diversity in what is assessed. Some instruments measure communication apprehension. Others test the students' knowledge of principles of communication or the student's ability to recognize standard English usage in written passages. Such measures tell us what a student may feel or know about communication, but they do not tell us what a student can do.

Second, most instruments isolate speaking from listening. The most common means of assessing listening is a multiple-choice paper-and-pencil test; literal comprehension is emphasized in these measures. Performance rating scales are the most common means for assessing speaking skills. Separate measures for speaking and listening may be necessary from a psychometric standpoint, but when one considers that testing influences teaching, there is a possibility that oral communication instruction will stress separate rather than interactive skills.

Third, assessment instruments must match instructional goals. Ready-made instruments may deviate from goals that a school system has identified as important. When some colleagues and I (Brown, et al., 1979) compared the skills tested by existing instruments with those that had been specified for the Massachusetts basic skills program, we found no tests that sufficiently matched our goals.

Fourth, reliability and feasibility of measurement present problems, particularly when assessing speaking skills. Few existing measures report test-retest reliability; some vary the topic of talk without establishing equivalence of topics; and some performance rating procedures have not attained high levels of agreement among different raters. Feasibility problems arise when measures require too much equipment and time.

A fifth problem is the possibility of bias. The context in which the test is administered, the stimulus situation, and the response mode are potential sources of bias in a performance test of speaking and in an objective test of listening. In addition, rater bias can threaten test score dependability in speaking performance assessment, but can be avoided through careful specification of performance criteria, careful selection of raters, and thorough rater training (Stiggins, 1981).

What is being done to address these problems? Current practices include monitoring assessment efforts in various states (Backlund, et al., in press), and developing new instruments. With regard to this last practice, some state and local education agencies are developing their own criterion-referenced means of assessing listening skills. Michigan, Massachusetts, and New Hampshire have developed listening tests, while Vermont offers guidelines for teachers to assess listening skills in classroom activities (Backlund, et al., in press). Performance rating scales are being developed to assess speaking skills. Hawaii (Backlund et al., in press) is developing a rating scale that assesses the student's oral communication competency in the day-to-day classroom situation. Massachusetts (1981) is developing a scale that assesses content, delivery, organization, and language skills in the context of four communication functions (giving directions, describing, persuading, and producing an emergency call). Glynn County, Georgia, has developed rhetorical trait scales to assess students' participation in a simulated public hearing and an employment interview (Rubin and Bazzle, 1981). Dickson (1981) and McCaffrey (1980) advise assessing oral communication through referential communication tasks. This advice is being pursued by Project Signals (1981).

As basic skills programs mature, additional assessment instruments need to be developed. Criteria that speaking and listening instruments ought to meet are discussed elsewhere (Brown, et al., 1979; Speech Communication Association, 1980), but a few guidelines follow.

For listening tests, stimulus materials should be relatively brief and should contain real-life spoken language used in situations that are meaningful to the students to be assessed. To control for possible administrative variation, the tests should be relatively self-contained on audio tapes. While test booklets and machine scorable response sheets may be used, the tapes should contain all stimulus materials—the spoken messages and the questions that elicit responses to the messages.

To assess speaking skills, a test with clearly defined criteria for evaluating performance should be used. Students should be assessed in familiar situations, preferably multiple ones, that emphasize purposeful communication. Only personnel who have been trained in administering the test and in judging performance should be responsible for assessment, and then only after they have demonstrated ability to judge performance reliably.

Summary and Recommendations

In the context of basic skills programs, I have addressed five concerns about oral communication instruction: instructional foci, sequencing, intervention effects, home-school cooperation, and assessment. My recommendations for each concern are as follows:

1. Instructional Approaches: Efforts to develop basic skills staff should include inservice training in different instructional approaches; their rationale and pedagogical assumptions; their methods and materials; their advantages and limitations; and their effects. Particular emphasis should be given to instruction

that facilitates the use of skills for functional effectiveness.

2. Instructional Sequencing: Since instructional sequences should be based on knowledge of the development of pragmatic communication, teachers and curriculum planners should be supported in their efforts to pursue continuing education aimed at understanding children's communication development. Inservice workshops, seminars, and courses should be provided to that end at the local and state levels. In addition, federal and private agencies should give a high priority to supporting research that investigates children's development of uses of language, and relates that development to curricular sequences.

3. Intervention Effects: Classroom teachers should teach oral communication directly as well as indirectly in both the elementary and secondary schools. Indirect intervention affords opportunity for practicing skills in a range of situations. Direct intervention promotes systematic acquisition of skills that are problematic for students.

4. Home-School Cooperation: School personnel should help parents become more conscious of their role as "the first teachers of oral communication" by preparing practical resource materials for use at home, securing practical library resources on parent-child communication, and including parents in curriculum planning efforts.

5. Assessment: Federal, state, and local education agencies should address assessment issues directly by developing new instruments and procedures that are valid, reliable, and feasible. In addition, these agencies should conduct cost-effectiveness studies to allay or confirm concerns that oral communication assessment is too time consuming and costly. The results of new assessment efforts should be disseminated widely throughout basic skills programs in order to promote alternative means of assessment and to avoid reinventing the wheel.

REFERENCES

Allen, R. R., and Brown, K. L. *Developing Communication Competence in Children.* Skokie, IL: National Textbook Co., 1976.

Allen, R. R., and Wood, B. S. "Beyond Reading and Writing to Communication Competence." *Communication Education,* 1978, 27, 286-293.

Allen, R. R., Parish, S., and Mortenson, D. *Communication: Interacting Through Speech.* Columbus, OH: Charles E. Merrill Publishing Co., 1974.

Allen, R. R., Willmington, S. C., and Sprague, J. *Speech Communication in the Secondary School.* (2nd ed.). Boston: Allyn and Bacon, 1976.

Asher, S. R., and Wigfield, A. "Training Referential Communication Skills." In W. P. Dickson (Ed.), *Children's Oral Communication Skills.* New York: Academic Press, 1981.

Bacon, W. A. *Oral Interpretation and the Teaching of Literature in the Secondary Schools.* Annandale, VA: Speech Communication Association, 1974.

Barbour, A., and Goldberg, A. A. *Interpersonal Communication: Teaching Strategies and Resources.* Annandale, VA: ERIC/RCS, Speech Communication Association, 1974.

Barclift, J., Blocker, D., Britton, B., Flowers, D., and Grant, J. *Child Talk.* Norton, MA: Project Signals, 1980.

Beyer, B., Lee, C., and Wilkinson, C. *Speaking of . . . Communication/Interpretation/Theatre.* Glenview, IL: Scott, Foresman and Co., 1975.

Bloom, B. S., Englehard, M. D., Furst, E. J., Hill, W. H., and Krathwohl, D. R. *Taxonomy of Educational Objectives, Handbook I: Cognitive Domain.* New York: David McKay Co., 1956.

Book, C. L. "Teaching Functional Communication Skills in the Secondary Classroom." *Communication Education,* 1978, 27, 322-328.

Book, C. L., and Galvin, K. *Instruction in and About Small Group Discussion.* Annandale, VA: ERIC/RCS, Speech Communication Association, 1975.

Book, C. L., and Pappas, E. J. "The Status of Speech Communication in Secondary Schools in the United States: An Update." *Communication Education,* 1981, 30, 199-209.

Braden, W. (Ed.). *Speech Methods and Resources.* (2nd ed.). New York: Harper and Row Publishers, 1972.

Brooks, W. D., and Friedrich, G. W. *Teaching Speech Communication in the Secondary School.* Boston: Houghton Mifflin, 1973.

Brown, K. L. "Applied Communication: Learning to Communicate in Interpersonal Situations. In R. R. Allen and K. L. Brown (Eds.), *Developing Communication Competence in Children.* Skokie, IL: National Textbook Co., 1976.

Brown, K. L., Backlund, P., Gurry, J., and Jandt, F. *Assessment of Basic Speaking and Listening Skills: State of the Art and Recommendations for Instrument Development.* Vols. I and II. Boston: Massachusetts Dept. of Education, 1979. (ERIC Document Reproduction Service Nos. ED 178 969 & ED 178 970).

Brown, K. L., Burnett, N. Jones, G., Matsumoto, S., Langford, N. J., and Pacheco, M. *Teaching Speaking and Listening Skills in the Elementary and Secondary School.* Boston: Massachusetts Department of Education, 1981.

Byrne, M. C. *The Child Speaks.* New York: Harper and Row, 1965.

Carlile, C. S. *Thirty-eight Basic Speech Experiences.* (5th ed.). Pocatello, ID: Clark Publishing Co., 1972.

Carlson, R. K. *Literature for Children: Enrichment Ideas.* Dubuque, IA: W. C. Brown, Co., 1970.

Cazden, C. B. *Child Language and Education.* New York: Holt, Rinehart and Winston, Inc., 1972.

Chambers, D. W. *Storytelling and Creative Drama.* Dubuque, IA: W. C. Brown, Co., 1970.

Delia, J. G., Kline, S. L., and Burleson, B. R. "The Development of Persuasive Communication Strategies in Kindergartners Through Twelfth Graders." *Communication Monographs,* 1979, 46, 241-257.

Dickson, W. P. "Referential Communication Activities in Research and in the Curriculum: A Meta-analysis." In W. P. Dickson (Ed.). *Children's Oral Communication Skills.* New York: Academic Press, 1981.

Dickson, W. P., and Patterson, J. H. "Evaluating Referential Communication Games for Teaching Speaking and Listening Skills." *Communication Education,* 1981, 30, 11-22.

Duke, C. R. *Creative Dramatics and English Teaching.* Urbana, IL: National Council of Teachers of English, 1974.

Ehrlich, H. W. *Creative Dramatics Handbook.* Philadelphia, PA: The School District of Philadelphia, 1974.

Ervin-Tripp, S., and Mitchell-Kernan, C. (Eds.). *Child Discourse.* New York: Academic Press, 1977.

Fishbein, H. D., and Osborn, M. "The Effects of Feedback Variations on Referential Communication of Children." *Merrill-Palmer Quarterly,* 1971, 17, 243-250.

Fletcher, J. E., and Surlin, S. H. *Mass Communication Instruction in the Secondary School.* Annandale, VA: Speech Communication Association, 1978.

Galvin, K., and Book, C. *Person-to-Person: An Introduction to Speech Communication.* Skokie, IL: National Textbook Co., 1981.

Glaus, M. *From Thoughts to Words.* Urbana, IL: National Council of Teachers of English, 1965.

Gleason, J. B. "An Experimental Approach to Improving Children's Communicative Ability." In C. B. Cazden (Ed.), *Language in Early Childhood Education.* Washington, D.C.: National Association for the Education of Young Chidren, 1972.

Glenn, E. C. "A Workshop for Speech Communication, K-6. *Communication Education,* 1978, 27, 343-346.

Glucksberg, S., Krauss, R., and Higgins, E. T. "The Development of Referential Communication Skills." In F. D. Horowitz (Ed.), *Review of Child Development Research* (Vol. 4). Chicago: University of Chicago Press, 1975.

Glucksberg, S., Krauss, R. M., and Weisberg, R. "Referential Communication in Nursery School Children: Method and Some Preliminary Findings," *Journal of Experimental Child Psychology,* 1966, 3, 335-342.

Halliday, M. A. K. *Learning How to Mean: Explorations in the Development of Language.* New York: Elsevier, 1977.

Haynes, J. L. *Organizing a Speech: A Programmed Guide.* Englewood Cliffs, NJ: Prentice-Hall, 1973.

Henry, M. W. (Ed.). *Creative Experiences in Oral Language.* Urbana, IL: National Council of Teachers of English, 1967.

Higgins, E. T. *A Social and Developmental Comparison of Oral and Written Communication Skills.* Unpublished doctoral dissertation, Columbia University, 1973.

Hopper, R., and Naremore, R. J. *Children's Speech: A Practical Introduction to Communication Development.* New York: Harper and Row Publishers, 1978.

Hopper, R., and Wrather, N. "Teaching Functional Communication Skills in the Elementary Classroom." *Communication Education,* 1978, 27, 316-322.

Krathwohl, D. R., Bloom, B. S., and Masia, B. B. *Taxonomy of Educational Objectives, Handbook II: Affective Domain.* New York: David McKay Co., 1964.

Krauss, R. M., and Glucksberg, S. "The Development of Communication Competence as a Function of Age. *Child Development,* 1969, 40, 255-266.

Larson, C., Backlund, P., Redmond, M., and Barbour, A. *Assessing Functional Communication.* Annandale, VA: ERIC/RCS, Speech Communication Association, 1978.

Lieb-Brilhart, B. "The Relationship Between Some Aspects of Communicative Speaking and Communicative Listening." *Journal of Communication,* 1965, 15, 35-46.

Lindfors, J. W. *Children's Language and Learning.* Englewood Cliffs, NJ: Prentice-Hall, 1980.

Loban, W. "Language Development and Its Evaluation." In A. H. Grommon (Ed.), *Reviews of Selected Published Tests in English.* Urbana, IL: National Council of Teachers of English, 1976.

Lundsteen, S. W. *Listening: Its Impact on Reading and the Other Language Arts.* Urbana, IL: National Council of Teachers of English, 1979.

Johnson, F. L. *Role-Taking and Referential Communication Abilities in First and Third-grade Children Contrasted in Birth Order Positions in the Family.* Unpublished doctoral dissertation, University of Minnesota, 1974.

Mackintosh, H. K. (Ed.). *Children and Oral Language.* Washington, D.C.: Association for Childhood Education International, 1964.

Massachusetts Department of Education. *Massachusetts Assessment of Basic Skills: Listening-Speaking Overview.* Boston: Author, 1981.

McCaffrey, A. *Testing Model of Communicative Competence in the Classroom.* Final report. (NIE Project No. G-76-0042). Washington, D.C.: National Institute of Education, 1980.

Moffett, J. *A Student-Centered Language Arts Curriculum, Grades K-13: A Handbook for Teachers.* Boston: Houghton Mifflin, 1968a.

Moffett, J. *Teaching the Universe of Discourse.* Boston: Houghton Mifflin, 1968b.

Newcombe, P. J. *Communicating Message and Meaning.* Boston: Ginn and Co., 1980.

Newcombe, P. J., and Robinson, K. F. *Teaching Speech Communication.* New York: David McKay Co., 1975.

Patterson, C. J., and Kister, Mary C. "The Development of Listener Skills for Referential Communication. In W. P. Dickson (Ed.), *Chidren's Oral Communication Skills.* New York: Academic Press, 1981.

Pipho, C. "Minimum Competency Testing in 1978: A Look at State Standards." *Phi Delta Kappan,* 1978, 59, 585-588.

Pipho, C. *State Activity: Minimal Competency Testing.* Unpublished paper, Denver, Co: Education Commission of the States, 1979.

Prentice, D., Pollard, T., and McComas, P. (Eds.). *Speech, Drama, and Mass Media: Practical Activities for Classroom Teachers.* Lawrence: University of Kansas, 1979.

Project Signals. "Student Objectives." Unpublished paper, Norton, Massachusetts, 1981.

Rubin, D. L. "Using Performance Rating Scales in Large-Scale Assessments of Oral Communication Proficiency." In R. J. Stiggins (Coordinator), *Perspectives on the Assessment of Speaking and Listening Skills for the 1980s.* Proceedings of a symposium presented by Clearinghouse for Applied Performance Testing, Portland, OR: Northwest Regional Educational Laboratory, 1981.

Rubin, D., and Bazzle, R. E. *C.B.E.: Development of an Oral Communication Assessment Program—the Glynn County Speech Proficiency Examination for High School Students.* Brunswick, GA: Glynn County School System, 1981.

Rubin, D. L., Daly, J., Dickson, W. P., McCroskey, J. C., and Mead, N. *A Review and Critique of Procedures for Assessing Speaking and Listening Skills Among Preschool Through Grade Twelve Students.* Annandale, VA: Speech Communication Association, in preparation.

Russell, H. D., and Russell, E. F. *Listening Aids Through the Grades.* New York: Teachers College Press, 1979.

Shantz, C. U. "The Role of Role-Taking in Children's Referential Communication." In W. P. Dickson (Ed.), *Children's Oral Communication Skills.* New York: Academic Press, 1981.

Speech Communication Association. *Resources for Assessment in Communication.* Annandale, VA: Author, 1980.

State of Illinois. *Basic Oral Communication Skills: A Program Sequence for Illinois Schools.* Springfield: Author, 1981a.

State of Illinois. *Parents as Teachers: Helping Your Children to Become Better Communicators.* Springfield: Author, 1981b.

Staton-Spicer, A. Q., and Bassett, R. E. "A Mastery Learning Approach to Competency-Based Education for Public Speaking Instruction." *Communication Education,* 1980, 29, 171-182.

Stiggins, R. J. "Potential Sources of Bias in Speaking and Listening Assessment." In R. J. Stiggins

(Coordinator), *Perspectives on the Assessment of Speaking and Listening Skills for the 1980s.* Proceedings of a symposium presented by Clearinghouse for Applied Performance Testing. Portland, OR: Northwest Regional Educational Laboratory, 1981.

Tough, J. *The Development of Meaning.* New York: Wiley, 1977.

Wells, G. *Coding Manual for the Description of Child Speech.* Bristol, England: University of Bristol School of Education, 1973.

Whitehurst, G. J., and Sonnenschein, S. "The Development of Informative Messages in Referential Communication: Knowing When Versus Knowing How." In W. P. Dickson (Ed.), *Children's Oral Communication Skills.* New York: Academic Press, 1981.

Wood, B. S. *Children and Communication: Verbal and Nonverbal Language Development.* (2nd ed.). Englewood Cliffs, NJ: Prentice-Hall, 1981.

Wood, B.S. (Ed.). *Development of Functional Communication Competencies: Pre-K—Grade 6.* Annandale, VA: ERIC/RCS, Speech Communication Association, 1977a.

Wood, B. S. (Ed.). *Development of Functional Communication Competencies: Grades 7-12.* Annandale, VA: ERIC/RCS, Speech Communication Association, 1977b.

PART VI:
NEW DIRECTIONS AND NEW ROLES
IN THE BASIC SKILLS MOVEMENT

THE QUEST FOR SUCCESSFUL BASIC SKILLS PROGRAMS: FOCUS FOR THE 1980s

Shirley A. Jackson
U.S. Department of Education

While quests for effective basic skills programs have been conducted in this country for a long time, no panacea for our many educational problems has been found. But we *are* starting to solve some of our problems, and despite press coverage to the contrary, the increased educational achievement of most of the students in this country can be documented:

1. In every sector of the nation achievement scores of elementary students (especially at the primary level) have gone up. Based on this evidence, it is safe to say that we have some sound strategies for teaching beginning reading in this country.
2. The national Assessment of Educational Progress showed an average gain for 17-year-old in-school youth of more than two percentage points on basic reading items between 1971 and 1975.
3. The same study showed that 9-year-old children—white and black, North and South—have improved in the basics of reading, writing, and math. The assessment found the most striking gains among nine-year-old black children in the Southeast. This is significant because that is where the Federal government has spent most of its education dollars—helping younger children from poor families in the early years of schooling.
4. State competency examinations in Michigan, Indiana and Florida (to name a few) show marked improvement in student achievement.
5. More students, black and white, complete high school. In 1900 about 6 percent of youth completed high school; now 80 percent do, and about half of those go on to further education.
6. Evidence from Army tests and the Iowa Test of Basic Skills indicates that indicates students' literacy, knowledge, and skills are higher today than they were forty years ago.

We have made, then, some significant progress in achieving our educational goals in this country. And, as I want to suggest next, we have also learned a great deal about how to further our ongoing quest for successful basic skills programs.

Research during the past decade has led the way in suggesting what works in basic skills instruction. Consider the findings of some representative research studies which sum up much of what we know about achieving success in the basic skills.

The "school effectiveness" studies of Edmonds and Lezotte refute previous studies which identified socioeconomic status as the prime determinant of basic skills achievement. These earlier studies often concluded or implied that schooling is ineffective and unproductive for poor children, as Coleman, Jencks, Jensen, and Schockly have pointed out. But "school effectiveness" studies now show hope; there *are* schools that are instructionally effective for low socioeconomic students. Such schools share five characteristics:

1. Strong instructional leadership is exerted, most often by the principal.
2. An orderly, positive school climate is evident.
3. Specifying objectives in the basic skills is emphasized. Objectives are then carefully monitored for mastery.
4. Teachers believe that *all* children can learn the basic skills. High expectations for success are applied to both students and teachers.

5. Assessment is an integral part of the program, and results are used not only for accountability but to improve instruction.

Any district interested in school improvement for the poor should seriously review all five characteristics and consider their implementation.

Research has not only pointed to the characteristics of effective schools, but it has also identified instructional variables associated with effective teaching. Specifically, the work of Brophy and Good, Bloom, Carroll, Block, Cohen and Stallings shows that the following variables are associated with effective instructional programs:

1. The program determines what is to be taught based on an identified developmental scope and sequence and identified standards of achievement.
2. The program diagnoses students' instructional levels as well as strengths and weaknesses in relation to objectives and standards.
3. The program develops instructional plans and strategies to meet the need of each child to develop concepts or skills. "Covering" chapters or pages is not an end in itself.
4. The program coordinates direct instruction and independent practice at the appropriate skills-development level of each student. Students understand the purpose for the learning activity assigned and see the connection between the skills being presented and the need to obtain functional, utilitarian literacy skills.
5. The program requires of students maximum time on assigned tasks and maximum *direct* instructional interaction time between teachers and students.
6. The program uses varied materials to develop concepts and skills. These materials reflect a consistency of methods and are used in accord with their author's design.
7. The program develops skills systematically, sequentially, and meaningfully with mastery as a goal.
8. The program insures that skills learned are immediately applied. (In reading, for example, there is an emphasis on reading for enjoyment and information).
9. The program integrates skills in reading, writing, and oral communication instead of teaching these as isolated, separate subjects.
10. The program systematically interrelates tests, instruction, and materials to reinforce each other. (Children are not tested on one concept, instructed on another, and assigned materials on yet another.)
11. The program has a management and record keeping system which continuously monitors the progress of each child. This system acts as a diagnostic and summative evaluation instrument which highlights pupil achievement and needs.
12. The program's teachers believe each student *can* master the objectives, and they seek the cause of failure in the instructional program, not the student.
13. The program is well-coordinated. Instructional consistency is maintained between intervention programs (Title I, Special Education, etc.) and classroom teachers' programs. Resource personnel (e.g., paraprofessionals, aides, volunteers) are trained to assist the teacher before they are placed in the classroom, and their training is coordinated with the classroom teacher's instructional goals and programs.
14. The program encourages parent involvement. Decision making is shared, and parents reinforce instruction. Communication with parents regarding pupil progress (positive as well as negative) is frequent.

15. The program uses an effective sequence of instruction.

This last point is important and warrants further explanation, for research shows that a specific instructional sequence does seem to yield the greatest benefit. This sequence includes eight steps. First, the knowledge and skills acquisition of students should be assessed in order to place them on the appropriate instructional level. Second, teachers should present material by direct teaching, showing *what* they expect students to know and *how* to learn it through a step-by-step process. Third, teachers should give *guided practice,* checking and correcting the students' work. They should also provide a variety of sample materials and situations, guiding students through these. Fourth, teachers should give *independent practice* and application, check and correct, assign additional material for independent practice, correct and review these, and then reteach. Fifth, teachers should assess the level of student mastery and the areas in which to reteach. Sixth, teachers should reteach, if necessary, or move forward on the developmental continuum. Seventh, teachers should offer periodic reinforcement of the skills and concepts taught; unless this is done, the time spent teaching will be wasted. Eighth, teachers should offer positive reinforcement and encouragement (a "you-can-do-it" attitude) throughout the sequence of instruction. This encourages students to expand and to enrich the skills and concepts they have learned.

All the foregoing research findings contain one common dimension—the teacher is seen as *the* critical element in a student's learning process. The *quality* of a teacher's instruction and classroom management makes a difference in his or her ability to teach basic skills effectively.

Aware of a few of our past successes and the direction provided by recent research, let us consider the future of basic skills education in the next decade.

Specifically, I wish to outline what I see as six areas of critical need for the 1980s. They are as follows:

1. Making all schools and teachers consistently effective in their delivery of instruction to poor and linguistically different students, improving the literacy levels of low-literate adults (the parents of many of these children), and helping these parents to help their children succeed in school.
2. Developing comprehension skills, especially higher-level thinking skills, in the middle and upper grades in the high schools. This should be done with an integrated basic-skills-across-the-curriculum approach, and not merely with isolated exercises in individual classrooms.
3. Developing viable writing and oral language assessment and instructional models, especially at the middle and upper levels.
4. Coordinating and integrating basic skills content instruction at the high school level, and coordinating and integrating basic skills programs funded by varied sources—federal, state, and local (such coordination to be achieved through joint assessment, planning, instruction, materials sharing, staff development, and evaluation).
5. Getting what we already know about successful basic skills programs *into practice* in all the schools and classrooms of this nation and extending our knowledge of what works.
6. Restoring public confidence in the school's ability to deliver quality basic skills programs.

Just as I see the above areas as critical during the next decade, I also believe that a number of specific questions should be asked about schools during the 1980s. Here are a few of those questions:

- Which schools teach which basic skills uncommonly well?
- Which schools teach basic skills poorly, if at all?

- What effective instructional innovations at two or more schools could be disseminated to an entire school system?
- Which approaches are some schools clinging to in spite of overwhelming evidence that they don't work? How would we rate the principals of those schools? Good? Bad? Indifferent?
- Are there schools serving essentially similar populations which do a significantly better job? Why?
- Do any or all of the local elementary schools use certain instructional methods for teaching reading? Does this seem to make any difference? Which approaches seem to work better for what sort of children?
- Which schools in the less affluent parts of town routinely surpass their companion schools in math and reading achievement? Is this difference the result of an outstanding principal or an easily adopted textbook?
- Is there a positive correlation between achievement scores and the amount of homework assigned?
- Are there observable differences among teachers regarding the ease with which they handle their subject matter?
- What are the successful techniques for establishing the classroom management and the discipline and order that make learning possible?
- What are the roles of the various testing programs (competency tests, standardized tests, teacher-made tests, etc.) in instructional improvement?
- What are the best ways to get schools to use the results of research in developing an instructional philosophy and designing, implementing, and evaluating programs?

These, then, are the needs and questions for the 1980s. But what help can we expect to find in fulfilling these needs, in answering these questions? In the past, the federal government has provided much of the "risk capital" to help educators answer questions. Previously, federal money has allowed researchers, state departments of education, and local education agencies to take time out for a period of exploration, experimentation, and planning. And I would argue that much of the progress we *have* seen has come from the federal effort. I believe, in fact, that the achievement results found in the National Assessment of Educational Progress are directly related to the federal intervention effort. While I know it is not popular at this juncture to talk positively about federal intervention, I believe that the money used to help identify and to assist poor children helped raise achievement levels to a point where, as mentioned earlier, the greatest progress has been made among 9-year-old black children in the Southeast.

But I don't wish to dwell on the past, for we are now in a period of transition, a shift towards the New Federalism. I would like, therefore, to look ahead, to assess the future role of the federal government in helping us meet the educational needs of the 1980s.

The New Federalism will remove the federal government as a central figure in educational improvement, shifting the burden for program improvement, evaluation, problem solving, and the arbitration of differences to the local and state levels. This will provide a wonderful opportunity for state and local education agencies and the community to redefine their relationships in cooperative ways. These groups will have to participate as colleagues in defining a common agenda. They will have to work together on questions of curriculum and find ways to improve educational achievement—issues that affect and should engage the entire community.

The New Federalism will also encourage mutual alliances between schools and businesses and industries. Educators might explore the shared employment of teachers and administrators with business and industry, or encourage business and industry to sponsor vocational training programs to interrelate job skills with the basic skills. Businesses might also sponsor motivational activities, such as annual awards for teachers, administrators, or students. The emphasis, in any case, will be on cooperation, on private-sector involvement with education.

State and local people will enter these cooperative arrangements differently, I think, when they know that their decisions cannot be undercut by a rule, regulation or project monitor, and when they know, too, that their problems will not be resolved by outside intervention. In the future the federal government will encourage state and local governments to get together to plan their work and to resolve their disagreements, while making it clear that the federal government will not be waiting in the wings ready to act as judge and jury.

The new federal role in education may depend ultimately on what we do with the Department of Education. The current administration, believing there is *no* viable federal role in education, hopes to accomplish five major objectives:

1. To dismantle the U.S. Department of Education;
2. To reduce federal funding of education;
3. To return the Constitutional rights and responsibilities associated with educating the citizens (along with the decision-making authority to do so) to state and local governments;
4. To stimulate competition in the educational marketplace through some form of tuition tax credits; and
5. To simplify and to reduce the paperwork requirements which accompany federal funding by consolidating educational programs and reducing regulatory and reporting requirements.

The government has already consolidated thirty educational programs. Block grants will now go directly from the federal to the state governments, with 20 percent of the money kept by state education departments and the remaining 80 percent passed down to the local level. These changes may have a profound impact on institutions of higher education, as about 60 percent of the newly consolidated funds formerly went to such institutions. Those in higher education must therefore develop new skills and learn to work more directly with state and local people. No longer will the money flow directly from the federal government in discretionary grant programs.

Secretary of Education Terrel Bell has emphasized that he wants the U.S. Department of Education (or its successor) to switch from the role of funding educational programs to leading and offering "effective assistance to schools and colleges." In September, 1981, the Secretary created a National Commission for Excellence in Education. The seventeen-member Commission, which constitutes a cross section of the educational community, will explore the causes of the recent alleged decline of academic rigor and student achievement in the nation's school and colleges. Under the leadership of David Piermont Gardner, president of the University of Utah, the Commission plans to compare our school and college curricula with those of other countries and to study the relationship between academic standards at the college level and achievement in high school. The Commission will conduct hearings around the nation to collect testimony on how students can be encouraged to work harder and to dig deeper into academic subjects.

Other responsibilities assigned to the Commission are these: to find out what we now expect of students, to look at the changes in education and society that have affected achievement over the past generation, and to define the problems now standing in the way of greater academic attainment. Both Dr. Bell and Dr. Gardner emphasize that the end product of this inquiry is not to set national standards or minimal competency requirements, but to focus on academic excellence, to encourage states and local districts to raise academic standards.

In its work, the Commission will report on successful schools, perhaps diverting media attention from the now familiar horror stories which claim that the schools are failing, that students can't read or write, that teachers don't have the skills necessary to teach, and that administrators don't know how to administer. We need to direct our efforts toward finding, describing, and replicating educational successes, and away from merely cataloguing failures.

As the New Federalism shifts the burden to the local and state levels, we can expect dramatic changes. For one thing, there is going to be more "accountability," more pressure to show results. People are going to say "Show me something more than happy evaluations and smiling faces; show me that you have really accomplished something." With the demand for accountability and the reduction of risk capital at the federal, state, and local levels, the focus of the 80s is going to be on the quest for successful programs. Many of our earlier efforts were on development. But times are changing. Now when I go before a Congressional committee to defend my budget, one of the Congressmen always says, "Tell me, Dr. Jackson, exactly how many students are reading better because of these expenditures? I understand from constituents that the students are not able to write. Now tell me, what are we doing about that?" What the Congressman really wants to know is whether we are making progress with the money. And I believe there is going to be more of this close scrutiny, more concern about which instructional systems measurably increase student achievement.

Faced with the demand for accountability, we can no longer jump from one bandwagon to another; we have done enough of that. We must remember that there are no panaceas, no magic methods or materials. We must keep our past, our history, in mind as we move forward so that we do not repeat our mistakes and so that we can build on the foundation of our experiences.

BASIC SKILLS: A STATE PERSPECTIVE

Raymon Bynum
Texas Commissioner of Education

When I am asked, as Commissioner of Education, to look ahead and tell what is going to happen in the 1980s, I get the feeling that some people believe I have a crystal ball. I assure you that I don't; as a matter of fact, I find it rather difficult to report what happened last week. With this caveat in mind, let me describe briefly some recent trends in Texas education and *then* let me look ahead to the 1980s and outline for you three areas of emphasis.

During the 1970s in Texas education we were concerned primarily with providing equity in public education. Initially, some of us may have subscribed to the mistaken notion that everyone is equal. However, we have come to recognize that all of us are not equal—we have different talents and so on. What we must provide for all students, though, is clear—*equal educational opportunity.*

Since the 1970s we have tripled the public spending in Texas public education. Within the last six years we have added 20,000 professional personnel. Today, Texas has the lowest teacher-pupil ratio of any state with over one million pupils. Last year we employed 186,652 professional personnel in the public schools. They serve 2,800,000 students—one classroom teacher for every 16 pupils.

In 1969, 65 percent of Texans were Anglo. This year, for the first time, there were more minority pupils in the first grade than there were Anglo pupils. For example, we are adding between six and seven thousand Asian pupils per year and twenty-five to thirty-five thousand Hispanic pupils. Overall, we presently have a two percent influx of new people moving into Texas each year. In essence, we have a greatly changing population with different cultures, educational backgrounds, and desires. Unlike many other states, however, over 93 percent of all school-age pupils in Texas attend public schools. Wisconsin, by contrast, has over 20 percent of its school-age pupils attending private schools. So you can see that in Texas we still educate all the pupils of all the people.

Let us now turn to the 1980s. We are going to continue, in the 80s, to deal basically with finance. A speaker at a conference I recently attended summed up this concern quite well when he said that education was a federal concern, a state responsibility, and a local function. And, as we all recognize today, the federal government is daily becoming less concerned with education; the state cannot decide who is responsible; and the locals are just wishing the funds had been left so they could function.

Central to our efforts to improve basic skills instruction in Texas schools is, first of all, the development of a new curriculum to meet the needs of our ever-changing student population. A joint resolution was passed through the Texas legislature for the Texas Education Agency to develop an essential basic skills curriculum in twelve areas—English language arts; other languages, to the extent possible; mathematics; science; health; physical education; fine arts; social studies; economics, with emphasis on the free enterprise system and its benefits; business education; vocational education; and Texas and United States history as individual subjects and in reading courses.

In an attempt to define the essential elements of a good K-12 basic skills program, we are seeking the opinions of concerned teachers, parents, and volunteers from cities and towns around the state. At this very moment, for example, forty-five people concerned with what we may call the English-language arts cluster are meeting in Houston. These professionals, nominated by their peers across the state, will offer their suggestions for the language arts curriculum.

A second area that I will emphasize to improve basic skills instruction is teachers' salaries. It is well known that Texas has a problem in this area—our annual teacher salary is only about 88 to 89 percent of the national average. We are faced with a situation in which we must look at the total structure of how we pay teachers. In short, we are going to have to do something dramatic.

Throughout the state we have been losing annually about five percent of our teaching force for various reasons—people leaving the profession, retiring, and so on. This means that we need nearly 9,500 new teachers per year just to maintain the status quo. Then, to handle our average annual growth, I would estimate that we need an additional five to six thousand new teachers per year. In response to this need, I will do all that I can to create in Texas a teachers' pay scale that attracts, and retains, the most qualified, talented teachers possible.

A third and final area that I will emphasize in the 1980s is inservice training for teachers. Our entire approach to teacher inservice training must be re-examined. Of the 20 percent of block grant funds earmarked for the state level (about six million dollars), I am going to demand that all of it be put into programs that affect inservice education.

In sum, the development of a well-balanced curriculum, the creation of a pay scale to attract qualified and talented teachers, and the design and delivery of inservice education grounded in the needs of participants are three tasks that require our most immediate attention if we are to continue to improve basic skills instruction in Texas in the 1980s. I believe that Texas—and other states that similarly establish a high priority for these tasks—can move ahead in the 1980s to produce models of excellence toward which others may aspire. We owe our pupils, and ourselves, nothing less.

THE ROLE OF HIGHER EDUCATION IN IMPROVING BASIC SKILLS INSTRUCTION

William M. Bechtol
Southwest Texas State University

I've been working in public schools and universities for almost 30 years. During this time I've been a classroom teacher, a principal, a central office administrator, a teacher educator, and a university administrator. As a result of these experiences, I've developed two fundamental beliefs about schooling. These beliefs affect my thinking about education and my present work in establishing school-university partnerships for the purpose of helping students attain basic skills.

First, schools exist for children. All that is done to establish and to maintain schools must be measured in terms of what is best for the child. This belief affects how one works in the teaching profession. For my own chidren and for all students, I want teachers and principals who believe that students come first.

Second, children, like fingerprints, are all different. If a teacher teaches for 40 years, a fairly long teaching career, that teacher will never have two students in his/her classes who are exactly the same. These individual differences among students are why educational problems are so complex. This means that there are no simple solutions that will solve the problems of improving student attainment of basic skills. Schools must be organized to enhance the uniqueness of the students and not to try placing them in situations in which all students are treated the same. Nothing is more unequal than the equal treatment of unequals.

These two beliefs—that schools exist for students, and that the individual differences of students make solving educational problems complex—influence my thinking and leadership in basic skills.

Concerns About Basic Skills

Basic skills instruction has been a concern of American educators for the three decades that I have been teaching. Even though achievement scores of elementary students have gone up across the nation—and there is some evidence that our schools are doing well—there is a concern. When I speak at a Rotary Club, I often have employers who are concerned with the number of their employees who have inadequate skills in reading, writing, and mathematics. They will ask me if we could help their employees learn to read better. That's a sad commentary on our graduates and one reason for the concern with basic skills. University leaders are concerned with the high number of students who are entering higher education with minimal or inadequate basic skills. This is a special concern of mine because many of these students don't know they have inadequate basic skills until they have difficulties in their freshman courses. Teachers, parents, and community leaders are concerned with the declining test scores of high school juniors and seniors. This concern has been publicized most by the media. Board members and school leaders are concerned with the increased number of dropouts that occur in schools that have implemented new competency standards. If someone says, "We've implemented new competency standards and more of our students are graduating with satisfactory skills, " check to see if the percentage of graduates has declined.

Many educators are concerned that the high public interest in the improvement of basic skills instruction will decline before adequate basic skills programs are in place. It is obvious that the federal support for basic skills is declining. Federal leadership in reading and basic skills will not continue. Responsibility for these programs will be passed on to the states. At the present, Texas has a great interest in the improvement of basic skills. The Texas Assessment of Basic Skills (TABS) test has been used with all third, fifth, and ninth graders since 1980. This testing has led most schools to implement better programs to improve basic skills instruction. But the concerns are these: Will there be the same interest in basic skills at the next legislative session? Will school district staffs continue their efforts to improve basic skills instruction? Is there a danger that states or local schools will lose interest in basic skills programs before adequate instructional programs are in place? These concerns led the staff of the Center for the Study of Basic Skills at Southwest Texas State University to sponsor the National Leadership Conference on Basic Skills. The purpose of the conference was to provide a forum for over 100 national leaders in basic skills. These policy makers used this conference to identify and discuss promising practices, problems, and solutions in basic skills instruction.

The Center for the Study of Basic Skills

Southwest Texas State University has a long history as an institution committed to teacher education. Since 1903, the university has progressed from a two-year normal school to a multi-purpose university of over 15,000 students. But the emphasis on teacher education remains strong. Southwest Texas State University now prepares more teachers than any other university in Texas. SWT's most distinguished graduate, President Lyndon B. Johnson, was always proud of his teaching credentials and his degree from a teacher education institution. It seems quite logical that the national leadership role in the improvement of basic skills instruction should emerge on the historic SWT campus.

The Center for the Study of Basic Skills was funded in 1978 under the University's Steeples of Excellence program. Initially, the Center included the Departments of Education and Mathematics. In 1979, the Department of English joined the original participants as an official member of the Center. Since that time, the Center has been staffed by faculty from these three academic departments. These are large departments with over 40 faculty members in each department. This year the Department of Speech Communication and Theatre Arts has joined the Center. The cooperation of four departments which are housed in four different schools illustrates the commitment of the faculty and administration of Southwest Texas State University to excellence.

The major goal of the Center is the identification of successful practices for the teaching of mathematics, reading, writing, and oral communication in elementary and secondary schools. The primary thrust has been to improve the teaching of basic skills from kindergarten through senior high. A secondary goal is to improve the teacher and administrative preparation program so that SWT graduates are professionals who can help students attain basic skills effectively. One special emphasis of the Center has been placed on the teaching of computer science as an emerging basic skill and as a fundamental tool for teaching other basic skills.

In the past four years the Center staff has had time and funds to study effective practices in basic skills. The staff has carried out research projects, visited many schools to assess needs and observe effective programs, developed a collection of basic skills curriculum materials, and disseminated findings regularly. The Center staff is particularly proud of the federally funded grant—The Southwest Texas Program for Improving Basic Skills Instruction in the Secondary Schools.

Also, Southwest Texas State University has been selected as the winner of the 1982 G. Theodore Mitau Award for Innovation and Change in Higher Education. This year the American Association of State Colleges and Universities selected SWT's Center for the Study of Basic Skills for its effective and innovative approach to an issue of great national concern: how to improve the teaching of basic skills at all levels.

Key Ideas in Teaching Basic Skills

Two years ago the Center staff identified the following research findings as the key ideas in teaching basic skills. I believe that a review of these ideas puts in perspective the papers presented at the National Leadership Conference on Basic Skills.

1. *Time spent in direct teaching is of the greatest importance if students are to master basic skills.* The frustrating thing about this idea is that it is so simple and logical. However, observers in classrooms have found that there is a tremendous difference between scheduled time and direct teaching. Much time in elementary classrooms is spent in non-teaching activities — collecting papers, lunch monies, discipline problems, etc. In secondary classrooms in addition to these non-teaching activities, students are out of class for other activities—baseball, school paper, FFA meetings, rodeo, etc. It's impossible for teachers to teach basic skills to students who aren't there. The need to increase the amount of scheduled time for students is not nearly as important as using the presently scheduled time more effectively. Well planned instruction with a high level of time on task promotes greater student learning. The amount of time spent in active teaching relates directly to increased learning gains.

2. *Students attain basic skills when their teachers expect them to achieve.* This key idea also sounds simplistic. But it's true. Teachers who expect their students to learn attain much greater results than teachers who do not believe their students will learn. Whatever we do in teaching depends on what we think students are like. Teachers who believe students can learn will try to teach them. A teacher who believes that a student is unable to learn may give up trying to teach him or her or spend days on a treadmill expending energy that will never matter. The teacher's expectation of how much a student will learn often becomes a self-fulfilling prophecy. Student achievement can be affected by changing the expectancy level.

3. *Good classroom management is required for teaching basic skills.* Teachers' managerial abilities relate positively to student achievement. Teachers who can structure, maintain, and monitor student learning activities efficiently have a decided advantage in teaching basic skills. Efficient management practices instituted the first few days of school positively effect student learning for the entire school year. Basic behavioral guidelines should be communicated to students and followed consistently. Teachers in well managed classrooms have more time on task to teach basic skills.

4. *Good teaching makes a difference in student achievement of basic skills.* Results from the Texas Assessment of Basic Skills (TABS) test reflect this idea. In one large county, school districts with large minority student enrollments had the greatest difficulty in mastering basic reading, writing, and mathematics skills. But in other school districts with large minority student enrollments, mastery of basic subjects was high. Good teaching makes a difference. The most efficient teaching machine ever invented is the teacher. Research findings consistently indicate that there are teachers who are highly effective in teaching basic skills. Enthusiastic, skillful teachers are the backbone of an effective basic skills program. Behind all students who exit school proficient in basic skills are good teachers who guided them on their way.

5. *Older students who lack basic skills can be helped.* It's easy for teachers and administrators to classify students and not expect them to achieve. However, anyone who has taught for a few years has success stories. There are effective programs

available at all levels for older students who have limited skills in reading, writing, and English. High school composition laboratories, vocational training programs, university remedial programs, reading clinics, and adult basic education programs have all been successful for some students. Winston Churchill's advice, "Never give up. Never . . . never . . . never," is appropriate for all of us who work with older students.

Conclusion

The foregoing five research principles have tremendous implications for teachers and administrators who want to help their students master basic skills more effectively. It is just such a set of fundamental convictions and expectations that teachers must have if they are to be successful.

From our work with the public schools in the Southwest Texas State University area, we have learned that these five research findings, though deceptively simple, are not easily implemented. It takes hard work, a professional and dedicated faculty, and sensitive administrators to put these findings into practice at any school. However, this is the sort of effort that is needed in the 1980s if we are to ensure that all our students attain the basic skills.

PART VII:
SELECTING INSTRUCTIONAL MATERIALS

QUALITY OF EDUCATIONAL MATERIALS:
A MARKETING PERSPECTIVE

Carol B. Daniels
LINC Resources, Inc.

The future of education is filled with challenges. Not only does the present economic climate cause education to complete more with other sectors of the economy for available funds, but the various factions within the education community are competing also for decreasing funds. With the shift to block grants for basic skills and the resulting responsibility at the state level for allocation of federal funds for basic skills, there is much confusion and political maneuvering on how to make available and spend block grant funds. Additionally, there is concern about the limited amount of funds available to purchase books and instructional materials, as well as about the quality of materials available commercially. Then, too, new technology in the form of microcomputers and software is vying for school budget dollars. Thus, not only is the aggregate budget for education smaller, but there are now more options for expenditure of funds for instructional materials.

The concern about the amount of funds available to purchase books and instructional materials stems from the fact that even when there were more funds available to purchase these items—such as funds from Title IV-B of the Elementary and Secondary Act—the latest data show that only 0.7 percent of the school budget was spent for these items in 1980. That means, for a typical school district spending $2,400 per child for education, only $19 was allocated for the purchase of books and other instructional materials. In a statement submitted to the Federal Commission on Excellence in Education, the Association of American Publishers stated, "to the extent that the quality of instruction is dependent upon a reasonable supply of up-to-date books and instructional materials, conditions in today's schools are growing steadily worse."

The concern about the quality of materials available commercially stems from the fact that the materials are the mainstay of the curriculum for most teachers— even though many educators are questioning the wisdom of relying on materials that they think have many shortcomings.

Educators indicate that some of the shortcomings existing in present commercially available materials are centered in teachers' manuals, readability levels, and workbooks. For instance, educators concerned with teaching reading are questioning how those responsible for teachers' manuals make decisions about what will be taught and when; they also question why practice is relied on for instruction rather than direct teaching, followed by appropriate practice. Educators note that the readability level often varies within textbooks; two texts that appear equally appropriate in terms of content coverage and degree of difficulty may be quite different with respect to readability variation. Concern about the quality of workbooks that are used to accompany texts is being expressed also. Educators point out that many workbooks have ambiguous and unclear directions; often, the exercises in the workbooks do not relate to what is supposed to be taught.

The influence of commercially available materials is powerful. According to a survey conducted by the Educational Products Information Exchange (EPIE) Institute, over 12,000 teachers of grades K-12 report that commercially purchased instructional materials are used during 90 to 95 percent of all classroom time. These teachers also report that if the materials they are using were suddenly unavailable, they would opt to use other similar commercially available instructional materials rather than do without.

Publishers of educational materials have a tremendous impact on what occurs in the classroom. By the time instructional materials reach the classroom, many important decisions have been made already by the publisher about curriculum in general, and about how instruction in a particular material will be arranged—such as decisions about the goals and objectives of the material; decisions about the scope and sequence of content; decisions about which specific teaching and learning activities will be contained in the material to stimulate learning of the content; and decisions about ways of assessing the learner's progress through and mastery of the material.

The fact that computers and software are very definitely going to be a part of the school world reinforces the need for educators to exert influence on publishers of educational materials. If publishers are convinced that educators will continue to buy materials presently available, publishers might be prone to produce these same materials in new electronic packaging.

Publishers agree that shortcomings do exist. However, they point out that most educational products are produced for a national market, and decisions about what to publish must be based on marketing considerations. Most publishers are sincerely concerned with educational quality and relevance, and many of them rely on market research—asking teachers what they want and what they will buy. But the bottom line is that many teachers and others do not know how to make wise selections and therefore continue to buy what is familiar rather than make critical judgments about products under consideration; therefore, publishers will continue to produce the best product they can sell rather than the best product they can devise.

Regardless of what curriculum guides say on paper, school districts must come to terms with the commercially published textbooks, workbooks, and other print and nonprint materials that actually define so much of what learners experience and teachers are meant to teach in the classroom. Those involved in the selection of materials should have training in the criteria necessary to select materials, and they should insist on evidence that the materials actually do what they purport to do.

In most school districts, the selection of instructional materials is often delegated to one or a few individuals. In many elementary schools, it is the principal who selects the major materials. In some schools, the principal may delegate the responsibility for selection of materials to a curriculum consultant or a committee of teachers. Teachers do have very definite assets to contribute to the selection of materials—they know the ability levels of their students; they are aware of the reading vocabulary and the potential difficulties resulting from an inappropriate reading level; they have a feel for whether or not material will integrate well with the rest of the curriculum being taught; and they know whether or not the materials are likely to appeal to their students. But despite their potential for offering a positive contribution, teachers as a whole play an insignificant role in the selection of instructional materials.

In one survey, 45 percent of the teachers surveyed said they had no role in selecting materials, 30 percent spent less than one hour a year on selection, and 25 percent spent an average of 10 hours a year on the selection process. Repeated assessments of teachers' perceived needs have found that they want help in individualization and in selecting materials. Because teachers are often not aware of the full range of available materials nor of how to locate them, teachers would certainly benefit from additional training in selecting instructional materials. Also, they should be encouraged to rely on competent reviews, recommendations, summaries of evaluations, and selection guides.

The criteria for the selection of materials for instruction are many and varied, and there are various levels of decision-making in the selection of materials. Anyone wanting to pursue that subject in more depth should read one or all three books by Marda Woodbury. As a group, the books are entitled *Selecting Materials for Instruction*; separated into handbooks they are called *Issues and Policies, Media and the Curriculum,* and *Subject Areas and Implementation* (Libraries Unlimited, Inc., Littleton, Colorado, 1979).

Greater involvement in the selection of instructional materials would help to make educators more aware of their potential influence on the quality of materials that publishers offer. It is not enough for the experts to write papers and articles about what is needed and about what practices are best. Educators must be influenced to become more discriminating in their selection of instructional materials by refusing to purchase materials that are not validated and proven effective with learners. Only when publishers begin to see sales drop will they be forced to spend more time and effort to eliminate the shortcomings of present materials and then to be more selective as to future offerings.

Educators and publishers are encouraged to reassess present instructional materials—and then to take the time to determine how the ideals of the educators and the practicalities of the publishers can best be meshed to provide instructional materials that are relevant and useful for the best education for pupils in the 1980s.*

*This paper was produced by LINC Resources, Inc. through the Basic Skills Validation and Marketing Program, Funded by the Basic Skills Improvement Program, the U.S. Department of Education, Contract Number 300-80-0957. However, opinions expressed herein do not necessarily reflect the position or policy of the United States Department of Education and no official endorsement of the United States Department of Education should be inferred.

EPILOGUE

CONTINUING THE QUEST: LEADERSHIP FOR IMPROVING THE QUALITY OF SCHOOLING IN THE 1980s

Forrest W. Parkay and Sharon O'Bryan
Southwest Texas State University

As many of the papers in this volume have pointed out, hardly a day goes by that the media do not remind us anew of the fact that our nation's schools are not teaching all their students the basic skills. The literacy rate in the United States has dropped alarmingly during the last two decades, and, as a brief review of those 20 years indicates, the problem seems frustratingly beyond our best innovative efforts.

Since the 1960s, the federal government has spent hundreds of millions of dollars in its quest to improve schools. The results of these efforts, many observers would say, have been disappointing; others, like Paul Copperman (1980, p. 75), even contend that these reforms have actually contributed to the "decline" of reading, writing, and learning.

During the years following the Civil Rights Act of 1964, educational policy makers and the general public became increasingly aware that our nation's schools, in significant numbers, were failing to educate their students for meaningful participation in our complex society. The gravity of this failure was evidenced by the frequency with which educators, such as Charles Silberman (1970), came to refer matter-of-factly to the "crisis" situation in the schools and to call for a "remaking" of American education.

Responding in typically American fashion, Americans began to try to remake their schools by infusing great amounts of money into the educational system. We at first believed that equalization of academic achievement could be achieved by assuring that school districts had equivalent resources—buildings, equipment, and instructional supplies. After all, it was easy to assume that certain schools reflected below average achievement *because* of inadequate resources.

The foregoing assumption was directly challenged, however, by James Coleman's (1966) report on equality of educational opportunity. He found that differences in resources among schools were not that important; instead, differences in test results appeared to be related to differences in student backgrounds. The student's immediate peer group influenced academic achievement most strongly. In short, the more middle-class students in a school, the better the academic achievement of any given student.

Coleman's findings encouraged a massive effort to remake American society—to solve our country's social problems—via the schools. Somehow, the schools were to become the great equalizer of the conditions of men. The elimination of poverty, racism and segregation, crime, unemployment, and other social ills—rather than learning—became the schools' major tasks during the era of the Great Society.

In the midst of this effort, Christopher Jencks (1972) asserted that improving schools would not reduce differences in income among adults. To many, Jencks' findings seemed to say that schools "didn't matter"—that changes in curriculum and teachers' methods and materials would not result in increased student achievement.

Nevertheless, there is today a growing body of evidence that refutes the notion that "schools don't matter." Instead, we are beginning to discover just how schools *do* matter. Taken as a collection, the papers in this volume represent a compelling, convincing statement that *today* we possess adequate knowledge to improve dramatically basic skills instruction in the 1980s.

We know that properly run schools can increase student learning. The major differences between schools that are successful and those that are not is in the *quality* of their educational programs—not the *quantity* of their resources. Effective schools are characterized by several factors: strong, capable leadership by the principal; a school-wide emphasis on basic skills; a school climate that emphasizes order and learning; appropriately high teacher expectations for student achievement; and a clearly thought out system for assessing student progress.

The foregoing factors are confirmed in strikingly similar fashion by the authors of the papers in this volume. Ross Taylor, for example, convincingly describes the procedures used in Minneapolis to raise students' scores in mathematics concepts and computation a full year above national norms—the approach emphasizes a commitment to mathematics instruction, high teacher expectations, time on task, leadership, and a carefully developed instructional management system. Thomas Good, in his summary of the last ten years of educational research, identifies some of the major variables associated with student learning—teacher expectations, active teaching, and classroom management. And Shirley Jackson points out how the increased educational achievement of large groups of children in this country is positively correlated with teachers who believe students can master objectives, with adequate time for direct instruction and independent practice, with strong instructional leadership, and with an orderly, positive school climate.

A Direction for 1980s

Having discussed where we've been and what we've learned during our quest to improve instruction, let us suggest the direction we need to pursue in the 1980s. While there is no doubt that these are tumultuous times for educational finance, we need to move ahead with renewed energy to ensure that all pupils reap the benefits of what we presently know about increasing student achievement. And what we do know is that the *quality* of a teacher's instruction and classroom management makes a difference in student learning. Thus, our efforts in the 1980s need to focus more directly on improving the *quality* of teaching—not only increasing the *quantity* of teaching as is evidenced by our present concern with time on task and other similar concepts. Effective teachers are distinguished not only by the amount of time they spend on instruction but *how* they spend this time.

What, then, do we mean by *quality* in teaching? Quality teaching occurs when the teacher's actions are informed by a sensitive understanding of, and "feeling for," the many factors which influence the teacher-student relationship at any given moment. This understanding is clearly seen in the effective teacher who sensitively facilitates educative relationships and then directs these relationships toward desired learnings.

While we are unable to offer a set of ten easy-to-follow steps to ensure quality in basic skills instruction, there are five principles which ought to guide us in our quest for quality.

• Those concerned with basic skills—whether practitioners, policy makers, or researchers—must remember that educational problems are profoundly complex and, as such, are beyond the simple solutions which are often proposed. Educational problems are multidimensional—not unidimensional. There are, as our past efforts to improve basic skills instruction remind us, no panaceas.

• In line with the above, we must remember that there is no one right way to teach the basic skills, no one right way to achieve quality. We therefore encourage educators, regardless of subject area, to adapt the stance that Lloyd Kline urges reading educators to recognize—that "pluralism is preferable to uniformity." Single, simple answers (while perhaps appealing) are difficult to justify, as *the* problem varies from classroom to classroom, from school to school. Effective teachers use highly divergent methods, and then—to compound the problem—not even these teachers are effective with all students. Thus, we cannot say, for example, that increasing time on task alone will, in all instances, result in greater student achievement. Or that encouraging teachers to convey greater expectations of students will, *ipso facto,* lead to greater learning. Or that increasing efforts at classroom management. . . . What we can encourage all teachers to do, though, it to increase their understanding of the patterns of variables that influence student learning in their particular situations.

• Teachers, educational policy makers, and researchers must strive for a deeper understanding of classroom dynamics; efforts must be made to achieve conceptual clarity in our thinking about problems in basic skills instruction. Only then can teachers apply intelligently the findings presented in this volume. This, of course, is not easily done, but that should not deter us from trying to get teachers to think more carefully about *why* they do what they do in the classroom. We need to encourage teachers to grow professionally and to monitor and to examine their teaching behaviors.

• In the 1980s, we must encourage teachers to improve their decision-making skills as they search for their own most effective methods for teaching the basic skills. Teachers should learn to become problem solvers and decision makers rather than implementers of systems, programs, and materials. Teachers need to develop ways of making decisions on their own about what techniques, materials, and models or theories to apply in a particular situation.

• Finally, we must, during the 1980s, work for an educational system that not only fulfills the short-range goal of increasing student achievement in the basic skills but also the long-range goal of demonstrating to students how continuous, life-long learning can enable them to live more satisfactory, meaningful lives. The basics of knowledge and skill are only part of the "essentials" of education. We need to ensure that not only do our students read, write, compute, and speak well but that they learn, for example, to think logically, to understand and to apply scientific methods, to make informed decisions, and to use technology wisely and humanely.

The Challenge

As we continue the quest for quality education in the 1980s, perhaps a reappraisal of the definition of basic skills is in order. Too often educators have sought to promote this or that innovation without considering *toward what end* or for what larger, hopefully humane, purpose the new method was suited. Shortsighted remedies accomplish little. Without long range, thoughtful consideration we may end up in the same spot that the Greek King Tantalus occupied. Recall that, to pay for his misdeeds, Tantalus was condemned by Zeus to stand in Hades, burning with thirst, in chest-deep water that receded when he bent to drink. Perpetually suffering from hunger, he had fruit dangling above his head—but it slipped beyond his reach whenever he sought to pluck it. Harold Shane, author of *The Educational Significance of The Future* (1973), used the analogy of the story to wonder how in the world we have managed to put ourselves into a situation in which the better things get, the worse they become. Beware that as we work on conquering the basics we may be no closer to our goal of attaining the elusive fruit of quality.

To prepare students adequately to live in the future, then, we must teach additional basic skills such as those Lupica (1982) outlines: coping with change; anticipating alternative future developments; knowing how to learn; using computer, voice, and visual equipment; developing human relations skills; and learning effective citizenship skills. We must, as Lupica points out, educate students to study

105

future possibilities by making them aware of major issues and developments that are highly probable and by having them analyze the short- and long-range problems and opportunities these issues will raise. For as Alvin Toffler (1970) suggests, the habit of anticipation is more important than specific bits of advance information. Hence, learning how to locate, obtain, and employ information will give learners the process skills for thinking.

The ability to know how to learn, as Lupica (1982, pp. 120-21) makes clear in the following, is an essential basic skill that our students must acquire today if they are to solve the problems of tomorrow:

Knowing how to learn is a process skill, while knowing what to learn is a content skill. In the future, we will need individuals who have been trained to think rather than to remember. Increasingly, the information one learns in school may become dated, irrelevant, or useless. Further, students will not be able to memorize the vast amounts of information generated by extended computer capacities. . . .

Thus, our continuing effectiveness resides in our ability to learn how to find, obtain and use information resources which provide the latest data necessary for solving problems or taking advantage of opportunities. These process skills help learners think analytically and intuitively, which in turn helps them organize their thoughts, define problems, or opportunities, ask the proper questions to reach solutions, understand relationships and connections among materials, synthesize information in a holistic manner, and choose the best solution(s) among the alternatives. Process skills also provide the learner with the ability to observe and recognize inconsistencies in data, propaganda techniques, advertising strategies, and consumer product information.

This certainly expands the definition of basic skills from the content of computing, reading, writing and speaking to include the processes of thinking, analyzing and problem solving. A quality education must, of course, pursue both dimensions of excellence.

In summary, the challenge during the 1980s is to keep alive the quest to improve the quality of schooling for America's children. It is our hope that the 1980s will be remembered as the decade during which research-proven principles of effective instruction were implemented to give students basic educational skills to cope in a changing world.

REFERENCES

Coleman, J.S., et al. *Equality of Educational Opportunity.* Washington, D.C.: U.S. Government Printing Office, 1966.

Copperman, P. *The Literacy Hoax: The Decline of Reading, Writing, and Learning in the Public Schools and What We Can Do About It.* New York: Marrow Quill, 1980.

Jencks, C. *Inequality: A Reassessment of the Effect of Family and Schooling in America.* New York: Basic Books, 1972.

Lupica, L. "Skills for the Future," in Reed, L. and Ward, S. (eds.). *Basic Skills Issues and Choices: Issues in Basic Skills Planning and Instruction.* St. Louis: CEMREL, Inc., 1982.

Shane, H. *The Educational Significance of the Future.* Bloomington, Indiana: Phi Delta Kappa, 1973.

Silberman, C. *Crisis in the Classroom: The Remaking of American Education.* New York: Random House, 1970.

Toffler, A. *Future Shock.* New York: Random House, 1970.

PARTICIPANTS
NATIONAL LEADERSHIP CONFERENCE ON BASIC SKILLS

KATHERINE B. AGUON
Agana, Guam

ROSALINDA BARRERA
New Mexico State University
Las Cruces, New Mexico

WILLIAM M. BECHTOL
Southwest Texas State University
San Marcos, Texas

BEVERLY BIMES
The Lindenwood College
St. Louis, Missouri

JUDY BRAMLETT
Region VI Education Service Center
Huntsville, Texas

JUNE BREWER
Huston-Tillotson College
Austin, Texas

BARBARA LIEB-BRILHART
National Institute of Education
Washington, D.C.

KENNETH BROWN
University of Massachusetts
Amhurst, Massachusetts

MARTHA BRUNSON
Southwest Texas State University
San Marcos, Texas

LOWELL BYNUM
Southwest Texas State University
San Marcos, Texas

RAYMON BYNUM
Texas Education Agency
Austin, Texas

RICHARD CHEATHAM
Southwest Texas State University
San Marcos, Texas

OLEN R. CHURCHILL
Arkansas Department of Education
Little Rock, Arkansas

BEECHER CLAPP
Department of Education
Knoxville, Tennessee

JUNE I. COULTAS
Department of Education
Trenton, New Jersey

EMMIE CRADDOCK
Mayor
San Marcos, Texas

EMMET CRAWLEY
LINC Resources
Columbus, Ohio

JEANNINE CRILL
Tarrant County Junior College
Arlington, Texas

ROBERTA CURINGA
San Gabriel, California

JOHN DAVENPORT
East Texas State University
Commerce, Texas

CELESTIA DAVIS
Texas Education Agency
Austin, Texas

JEAN DAVIS
Southwest Texas State University
San Marcos, Texas

LEONARDO DE LA GARZA
Austin Community College
Austin, Texas

OSCAR DORSEY
Southwest Texas State University
San Marcos, Texas

JOHN EDGELL
Southwest Texas State University
San Marcos, Texas

ELIZABETH EGAN
Silver Burdett Company
Morristown, New Jersey

AUDREY ELLIOTT
Incarnate Word College
San Antonio, Texas

MASA-AKA N. EMESIOCHL
Trust Territory Office of Education
Saipan

ANNA FARR
Southwest Texas State University
San Marcos, Texas

JOSEPH R. FOSTER
Arkansas Department of Education
Little Rock, Arkansas

GEORGE FRANKLIN
Region I Education Service Center
Edinburg, Texas

SHIRLEY FRYE
Scottsdale Public Schools
Scottsdale, Arizona

VICTOR FUCHS
LINC Resources, Inc.
Columbus, Ohio

ALAN GAGNE
St. Edwards University
Austin, Texas

JAMES J. GARLAND
Southwest Texas State University
San Marcos, Texas

MARGUERITE GILLIS
Southwest Texas State University
San Marcos, Texas

MARGARET GLEASON
Region XVI Education Service Center
Amarillo, Texas

THOMAS GOOD
University of Missouri
Columbia, Missouri

NANCY GRAYSON
Southwest Texas State University
San Marcos, Texas

BARBARA GRIFFIN
Southwest Texas State University
San Marcos, Texas

MARCIA GUDDEMI
Southwest Texas State University
San Marcos, Texas

MONICA HAMPTON
Director, The Children's Collective, Inc.
Los Angeles, California

BEVERLY HARDCASTLE
Southwest Texas State University
San Marcos, Texas

NELLIE H. HARRISON
CEMREL, Inc.
St. Louis, Missouri

KATHARIN HEAD
University of Texas at Arlington
Arlington, Texas

MICHAEL HENNESSY
Southwest Texas State University
San Marcos, Texas

JOHN HILL
Southwest Texas State University
San Marcos, Texas

JOHN HUBER
Pan American University
Edinburg, Texas

BILLIE HUGHES
Southwest Texas State University
San Marcos, Texas

SHIRLEY JACKSON
U.S. Department of Education
Washington, D.C.

JAMES E. JOHNSON
Texas Woman's University
Denton, Texas

JON JONZ
East Texas State University
Commerce, Texas

STEPHEN JUDY
Michigan State University
East Lansing, Michigan

SANDY KERN
Austin Independent School District
Austin, Texas

JAMES C. KING
The University of Akron
Akron, Ohio

HERBERT J. KLAUSMEIER
University of Wisconsin
Madison, Wisconsin

LLOYD KLINE
International Reading Association
Newark, Delaware

JOHN KOENIGS
Media Systems
Dallas, Texas

NEVIN K. LAIB
Texas Tech University
Lubbock, Texas

CLAUDIA LAIRD
Southwest Texas State University
San Marcos, Texas

JOANN LANGE
Seguin, Texas

SHERRY MC MAHON
Houston Community College
Houston, Texas

FRANCES MC NAIR
San Marcos, Texas

RICHARD I. MILLER
Southwest Texas State University
San Marcos, Texas

BETTY MOORE
Southwest Texas State University
San Marcos, Texas

DORTHEY K. MOORE
Mississippi State University
Jackson, Mississippi

JOE MOORE
Southwest Texas State University
San Marcos, Texas

JEANETTE MORGAN
University of Houston
Houston, Texas

PAT MURDOCK
Southwest Texas State University
San Marcos, Texas

ED MYERS
CEMREL Inc.
St. Louis, Missouri

ROBERT NORTHCUTT
Southwest Texas State University
San Marcos, Texas

JEFF NORTHFIELD
Australia

SHARON O'BRYAN
Southwest Texas State University
San Marcos, Texas

RUBEN OLIVARES
Fort Worth, Texas

MARY OLSON
Southwest Texas State University
San Marcos, Texas

FORREST W. PARKAY
Southwest Texas State University
San Marcos, Texas

EMILY MILLER PAYNE
Austin Community College
Austin, Texas

DAVID PEARSON
University of Illinois
Champaign, Illinois

KYLE PERRIN
East Texas State University
Texarkana, Texas

ARTHUR PHILLIPS
Region IX Education Service Center
Wichita Falls, Texas

LINDA REED
CEMREL, Inc.
St. Louis, Missouri

AGNES RHODER
Huston-Tillotson College
Austin, Texas

ROSEMARY RICHARDS
Region XII Education Service Center
Waco, Texas

SOILA RODRIGUEZ
San Marcos Independent School District
San Marcos, Texas

CLIFFORD RONAN
Southwest Texas State University
San Marcos, Texas

HOWARD SCHEIBER
New Mexico State University
Santa Fe, New Mexico

TOM S. SCHROEDER
Ball State University
Muncie, Indiana

WILLIAM J. SEILER
University of Nebraska
Lincoln, Nebraska

C. HILDEGARDE SLOCUM
New Braunfels, Texas

SARAH SPARKS
Dripping Springs, Texas

MARGARET STEIGMAN
Tyler Junior College
Tyler, Texas

MEDORA AN STELTER
Region V Education Service Center
Beaumont, Texas

LOUIS TASSIONE
Ft. Worth, Texas

ROSS TAYLOR
Minneapolis Public Schools
Minneapolis, Minnesota

JACK TENNISON
Texas Luthern College
Seguin, Texas

JUDIE THELEN
Frostburg State College
Frostburg, Maryland

SHIRLEY TIEDT
New Braunfels, Texas

MICHAEL VIVION
University of Missouri at Kansas City
Kansas City, Missouri

B. ALLAN WATSON
Southwest Texas State University
San Marcos, Texas

CHARLES WEED
Regional Planning Center
Albany, New York

BILL WHITFIELD
Region XVIII Education Service Center
Midland, Texas

DON WILLIAMS
San Marcos Independent School District
San Marcos, Texas

HARRIET DOSS WILLIS
CEMREL, Inc.
St. Louis, Missouri

SUSAN WITTIG
Southwest Texas State University
San Marcos, Texas

BETTY WOLVERTON
Texas Luthern College
Seguin, Texas

MAUCY WOOD
University of Texas at El Paso
El Paso, Texas

ADDIE WOODARD
Kyle, Texas

STINSON WORLEY
Southwest Texas State University
San Marcos, Texas

KEITH WRIGHT
Yakima Public Schools
Yakima, Washington

WILLARD YOUNG
Southwest Texas State University
San Marcos, Texas

ABOUT THE AUTHORS

Rosalinda Barrera is presently working as a specialist in bilingual reading instruction for the Department of Educational Specialties, New Mexico State University, Las Cruces.

William M. Bechtol, Professor of Education and Chairman of the Department of Education at Southwest Texas State University, serves as co-director of the University's Center for the Study of Basic Skills.

Beverly Bimes, National Teacher of the year, 1980-81, is presently affiliated with the Master Teacher Institute at Lindenwood College, St. Louis, Missouri.

Kenneth Brown, former editor of *Communication Education,* is presently Professor of Communication Studies at the University of Massachusetts, Amherst.

Ramon Bynum has held a variety of teaching and administrative posts in Texas education and is now serving as Texas Commissioner of Education.

Carol B. Daniels, is a Marketing Specialist for LINC Resources, Inc. LINC assists in the marketing of products prepared in Federally Funded Basic Skills, Consumer Education and Special Education programs.

Shirley Frye, past director of the National Council of Teachers of Mathematics, presently works as a Mathematics and Science Coordinator for the Scottsdale, Arizona Unified School District.

Michael Hennessy, Assistant Professor of English at Southwest Texas State University, teaches courses in writing and literature.

Thomas Good, co-author of *Looking in Classrooms* and *Teachers Make a Difference,* is Professor in the Department of Curriculum and Instruction, University of Missouri, and Research Associate at the Center for Research in Social Behavior, University of Missouri, Columbia.

Shirley Jackson, past director of Right to Read and the Basic Skills Program in the United States Department of Education, is presently Acting Assistant Secretary for Program Operations, Department of Education, Washington, D.C.

Stephen Judy has served as editor of *English Journal* and is now Vice President of the National Council of Teachers of English. He is also Professor of English, and Director of the English Education Program at Michigan State University.

Lloyd Kline, author of more than fifty books and articles, is presently Director of Publications for the International Reading Association.

Barbara Lieb-Brilhart has served as Director of Educational Services for the Speech Communications Association and is presently with the Office of Dissemination and Improvement of Practice, National Institute of Education, Washington, D.C.

Sharon O'Bryan, co-author of *Middle School/Junior High School Evaluative Criteria,* is an Assistant Professor of Education at Southwest Texas State University where she teaches courses in secondary education.

Forrest W. Parkay, Project Director for the Southwest Texas Program for Improving Basic Skills Instruction in the Secondary Schools, is an Assistant Professor of Education at Southwest Texas State University where he teaches courses in secondary education and counseling and guidance.

David Pearson is co-editor of *Reading Research Quarterly* and co-author of *Teaching Reading Vocabulary* and *Teaching Reading Comprehension.* He presently is associated with the Center for the Study of Reading at the University of Illinois.

Ross Taylor is presently serving as Mathematics Consultant for the Minneapolis Public Schools.